THE AGE OF THE
PICTS

THE AGE OF THE

PICTS

W.A. CUMMINS

ALAN SUTTON PUBLISHING LIMITED

First published in the United Kingdom in 1995
Alan Sutton Publishing Ltd
Phoenix Mill · Far Thrupp · Stroud · Gloucestershire

Reprinted 1996

British Library Cataloguing in Publication Data

A catalogue record for this book is available from the British Library.

ISBN 0-7509-0924-2

Typeset in 11/12 Ehrhardt.
Typesetting and origination by
Alan Sutton Publishing Limited.
Printed in Great Britain by
Butler & Tanner, Frome, Somerset.

Contents

List of Illustrations

Acknowledgements

My greatest debt is to the generations of unnamed scribes, who committed the Irish annals and the *Pictish Chronicles* to writing and kept them up to date; to Bede, who recorded such a wealth of fascinating detail about the history of his own time; and to Adomnan, whose *Life of St Columba* describes one of the most crucial encounters in the history of Scotland. Defective these records may be, but without them there would be no history at all and the Picts would be as prehistoric as their ancestors who built the brochs and the souterrains. Along with the contemporary and near contemporary writers, pride of place must be given to W.F. Skene, who, more than a hundred years ago, gathered into a single volume an invaluable collection of source material relating to the early history of Scotland. Finally, I could never have attempted to write this book without the wealth of modern archeological and historical research, from Wainwright's *Problem of the Picts* (1956) to the present time.

On a more personal note, my family have given help and encouragement throughout the preparation of this book. Judy, Tig and Andrew have read and commented on the text, drawn my attention to books I might otherwise have missed, helped with Latin passages that were beyond my distant schoolboy understanding, and accompanied me on excursions to Pictish sites. The book would have been poorer without them.

Acknowledgements for the reproduction of photographs are due to the following: p. 2, English Heritage: copyright reserved; 67, 69 (top), 70 (top) and 71 (top), The Trustees of the British Museum: copyright reserved; 68, 69 (bottom), 70 (bottom), 71 (bottom), 72, 74, 75, 77 and 130, National Museums of Scotland: copyright reserved; 73, Cambridge University Collection of Air Photographs: copyright reserved; 80 and 139, Historic Scotland: Crown copyright reserved. All other photographs and line drawings are by the author.

CHAPTER 1

The Professor and the Pictophile

The Picts were the first British nation to emerge from the tribal societies of the late Iron Age. For five hundred years, from the fourth to the ninth century, they flourished and were the dominant power in the north. Then in what seems, looking back over more than a thousand years, a remarkably short period of time, the Picts as a nation simply ceased to exist. Their language went out of use and is now almost completely lost, and their place was taken by the burgeoning Scottish nation, which had started life in the west as a small colony of settlers from Ireland.

While the tribes of northern Britain were giving birth to the Pictish nation, those of the south were in a state of suspended animation under the all-embracing rule of the Roman Empire. Viewed from the north, these people had themselves become Roman, an alien people living beyond the wall. Hadrian's Wall itself was a symbol of that alienation, as potent in its time as the Berlin Wall and the Iron Curtain of recent memory. The people on the other side of the wall were the enemy. After three Roman invasions in no more than 130 years, there could be no illusions about that. The fact that the orders for these attacks came from Rome rather than London or York meant nothing to the people at the receiving end. All they knew was that the invading armies advanced on them from southern Britain, and southern Britain was therefore enemy territory.

By the fourth century the tide was turning. As the Picts grew stronger in the north, the Roman authority in the south grew weaker. During the fourth and fifth centuries, the Picts took to the sea, where there was no Roman wall to bar their progress, and made lightning strikes into the very heartland of southern Britain. As Roman military protection was gradually withdrawn, the stranded Britons decided to employ Saxon mercenaries to combat these attacks. This policy, soon bitterly regretted, was to have far-reaching repercussions and eventually gave rise to the two nations of southern Britain, the Britons (later Welsh) and the English.

Much has been written about the Picts in the last 40 years, since F.T. Wainwright assembled his team of specialists to write *The Problem of the Picts*, a book which has rightly become a milestone in Pictish research. The root of the problem is that the Picts belong almost entirely to the Dark Ages, that twilight

Hadrian's Wall, beyond which (to the right) lay enemy territory: view to the east from Cuddy's Crags (Photo: English Heritage).

zone between history and prehistory, where neither historian nor archaeologist reigns supreme and neither can dispense with the services of the other. Had the Picts disappeared a few centuries earlier, they would have been part of the prehistoric Iron Age and we would know much less about them. Indeed the problems that concerned Wainwright and his colleagues could not have been stated, let alone solved. Had they lasted a few centuries longer, the Picts would have left records of their own history in their own language, and we would know a great deal more about them.

Wainwright's philosophy for penetrating what he referred to as 'the gloomiest shadows of the Dark Ages' was that 'specialists of different disciplines, bringing different methods to the varied assortment of evidence, must pool their resources and tackle together the problems that none of them alone can solve'.[1] This philosophy has been widely followed, notably in two recent conferences,[2] and has resulted in considerable advances in our knowledge. But, in terms of the familiar proverb, while we have learnt a great deal about Pictish trees, it is still difficult for an outsider to find a good account of the Pictish wood. The reason for this is not far to seek. Wainwright, in stressing the need for specialist studies, also issued a dire warning to anyone who might attempt a general study of the Picts: 'so many reputations have been shattered that only the confident and the careless will today venture into this graveyard of rejected theories'. The warning has been well heeded!

The archaeologists and historians who bring 'the sweat of fieldwork and the slow and troublesome toil of intellectual enquiry'[3] to bear on the problems of the Picts are a devoted minority. The lure of the Picts, however, reaches far beyond this small band of professionals to a wider public, fascinated by the aura of mystery that seems to surround them. There is of course much in common between the academic problem and the popular mystery, but there is also a considerable difference in emphasis. A brief summary of some of the problems will serve to illustrate this.

Who were the Picts? To what extent were they the indigenous (aboriginal) inhabitants of northern Britain and to what extent were they Celtic or other incomers? What did they call themselves? Did they have a native name, of which *Picti* was the latinized form, or did they really paint their bodies as the Latin word suggests and as has been widely believed?

Related to these questions is the problem of their language. Was it a Celtic language related to the British (Welsh, Breton, Cornish) or Gaelic (Irish, Scottish, Manx) languages? Was it non-Celtic, perhaps even non-Indo-European, reaching back to some primitive prehistoric ancestral language? Or was it perhaps some combination of these?

What was the origin of the Picts? Can the slender historical record, aided by archeological investigations, tell us when and how the Pictish nation came into being?

Did they, or at least did their kings, adopt a system unique in Britain of succession through the female line?

What is meant by the symbols on the Pictish symbol stones? There is universal agreement that these stones are indeed Pictish, partly Christian and possibly partly pre-Christian. Why were they set up?

Then there is the Pictish silver, recognized as such by the symbols beautifully engraved on some pieces and inlaid with red enamel. Some of these are isolated finds, but others were found in hoards, as at Norrie's Law, where Pictish silver was associated with late Roman silver. What is the interpretation of such associations?

When was Christianity first introduced to the Picts and by whom? The chief contenders seem to be St Ninian in the fifth century and St Columba in the sixth. But what about St Darlugdach? What indeed! Who has even heard of St Darlugdach?

What caused the disappearance of the Picts from the pages of history, just as the record was beginning to fill out? Did Kenneth mac Alpin defeat them in battle? If so, contemporary records kept unusually quiet about it. If not, who did defeat them, or what else happened so that, to all appearances, they simply ceased to exist?

Sueno's Stone in Forres is the greatest of all the sculptured stones in Scotland. Is it in any sense a Pictish stone and, if so, what does it commemorate? Or is it perhaps a Scottish stone, maybe depicting, as some have suggested, the final defeat of the Picts by Kenneth mac Alpin?

Such are some of the problems of the Picts. The mystery of the Picts has two aspects. The first is the feeling that they are different from the other nations of Britain in rather special ways: that their symbols are unique, that their system of matrilineal succession sets them apart and that their language has its roots set deeper in the prehistoric past than any other. The second aspect of the mystery is that some of the problems seem so completely insoluble that they will remain for ever the province of armchair romance and speculation.

The mystery of the Picts, unlike the problem (or problems), is not a popular concept in academic circles. As Professor Leslie Alcock stated recently, while introducing his 'new idealogy' for Pictish studies, 'it is manifest that the Picts were not the mysterious, problematic nation of earlier idealogies', and 'one of the major limitations of earlier Pictish studies has been their dogmatic Pictocentricity'. 'A major aim of the new idealogy', he continued, 'is to break the bonds of this dogma. It must be affirmed that the Picts were a typical north-west European barbarian nation, accepted as such by their contemporaries.'[4] The proposed new idealogy produced an immediate and strong reaction. It seemed 'that there was a strong popular wish to retain the concept of the Picts as a peculiar, special and problematic people; that the mystery which is supposed to surround them forms part of their attraction'.[5] Commenting on this reaction, Alcock concluded that 'the common perception of the Picts, stemming right back to Bede, is a misconception which has acquired the status of a hallowed myth'.[6]

Who is being deluded? The professor or the pictophile? And is the professor really daring to suggest that Bede was the perpetrator of a mystery which never really existed?

Bede (673–735), the 'Father of English History', was a contemporary writer. He was of course a foreigner (from the Pictish point of view), and spent most of his life as a monk at Jarrow in Northumbria. His great *Ecclesiastical History of the English People*, written in 731, was immediately presented to King Ceolwulf for approval.[7] The Northumbrians and the Picts were neighbours across a boundary which had fluctuated from time to time but had become more or less stabilized along the Firth of Forth. One way or another, as friend or foe, the kings of the Picts and the kings of Northumbria had known one another for generations. Bede was in no position to make ill-founded allegations about the Picts. His readers would have recognized them immediately for what they were.

So what did Bede say about the Picts? The answer to this question has to be: not very much. His purpose was, after all, to write the history of the English Church. However, in setting the scene for his history, he first of all gave an outline account of the whole of Britain.

> At the present time there are in Britain, in harmony with the five books of the divine law, five languages and four nations – English, British, Scots and Picts. Each of these have their own language; but all are united in their study of God's truth by the fifth – Latin – which has become a common medium through the study of the scriptures.[8]

He then goes on to account for the origin of these nations: first the Britons who, 'according to tradition', came over from Armorica (Brittany). Then the Picts, of whom 'it is said' that they came over from Scythia (possibly meaning Scandinavia) in a few long boats and, having been driven by storms around the coasts of Britain, eventually found a safe haven in northern Ireland. On landing, they asked permission to settle, but were politely told that there was no land to · spare. The Irish did, however, suggest that they might find suitable land across the sea to the east, and even offered help in case they met with any resistance.

So the Picts crossed into Britain and began to settle in the north of the island, since the Britons were in possession of the south. Having no women with them, these Picts asked wives of the Irish, who consented on condition that, when any dispute arose, they should choose a king from the female royal line rather than the male. This custom continues among the Picts to this day.[9]

Later in the book, Bede gives an account of the mission of St Columba to the northern Picts, beginning in the year 565. The southern Picts, he wrote, 'are said to have abandoned the errors of idolatory long before this date and accepted the true faith through the preaching of Bishop Ninian'.[10]

Finally, on relations between the Picts and Northumbrians in the seventh and early eighth centuries, Bede is writing from personal knowledge and first-hand accounts. Here the light of true history shines briefly through the gloom of the Dark Ages and for a while dispels the problem of the Picts.

In summary then, Bede supplied us with three facts about the Picts and their early history, and three stories:

1   Their language was sufficiently different from Scottish (Gaelic) and British (Welsh) to be considered a quite distinct language.

2   They chose their kings not by patrilineal descent, as was common among the other nations of Britain, but 'through the female royal line'.

3   The conversion of the northern Picts was begun by St Columba in 565.

4   The Picts were supposed to have come by sea from Scythia.

5   Having omitted to bring any women with them, the first Pictish settlers were supposed to have married Irish wives.

6   The southern Picts were said to have been converted by St Ninian long before the arrival of St Columba.

As the perpetrator of a hallowed myth, Bede seems an unlikely suspect. He was a serious historian and maintained a clear distinction between fact and hearsay.

Whether or not Bede was responsible for it, an air of mystery does still surround the Picts, and indeed contributes in no small measure to their continuing popularity. Several decades of specialist papers, while they have resulted in the accumulation of much new knowledge, have done little to dispel the mystery. This book is written in the belief that the time is ripe not for a new idealogy, but for a new look at the whole Pictish story, for an assessment of the problem of the Picts as it stands today, and for a balanced review of the mystery.

CHAPTER 2

The Land of the Picts

Pictavia, as the land of the Picts was sometimes called, had been inhabited for thousands of years before the Picts themselves first came to the notice of the outside world, towards the end of the third century AD. Neolithic farmers had begun the task of clearing the land for cultivation by about 4000 BC, and the work had been going on ever since. Apart from changing the face of the countryside, these early farmers left many other traces of their activity, and it is with the aid of these that we are able to plot their progress in bringing the environment under control. For some two thousand years, stone axes were used for clearing the forest. Then, during the early Bronze Age, the heavier axe hammer came into use, along with the first bronze axes. Stone axes, axe hammers and related tools are almost indestructible, and are often turned up by the plough or discovered during building operations. Besides these movable artefacts, there are many archeological sites: burial places (Neolithic chambered cairns and Bronze Age round barrows), religious sites (stone circles) and defensive works (forts, duns and brochs). All these and more are scattered about the countryside, some well preserved and others in varying stages of decay, but generally recognized and mapped. The combined distribution of these various objects and structures provides a good illustration of the land as it was at the beginning of the Pictish period.

The map is a revealing one. Its most striking feature is the fact that more than half the country seems to have been virtually untouched by human hand for four thousand years. The largest inhabited areas were in the eastern half of the country, while traces of human activity in the west are restricted to a narrow coastal strip. The reason is of course well known: the North West Highlands and the Grampian Mountains extend in an almost unbroken mass from the far north right down to the Clyde Estuary. Contact between the great eastern centres of population and the west was probably most easily maintained by sea, past John O'Groats and Cape Wrath. Apart from this, there was only the narrow and dangerous pass through the Great Glen, along the shores of Loch Ness and Loch Lochy. From the geographical point of view, there is no obvious reason why the people of the west coast should ever have been part of the Pictish nation, centred, as it certainly was, in the east. A political and cultural link with the Scots (Irish) across the sea might well have been more natural.

Looking more closely now at the eastern half of the country, it will be seen that an area with very little sign of prehistoric activity extends eastwards towards the coast between Aberdeen and Stonehaven. This represents the 'range of steep and

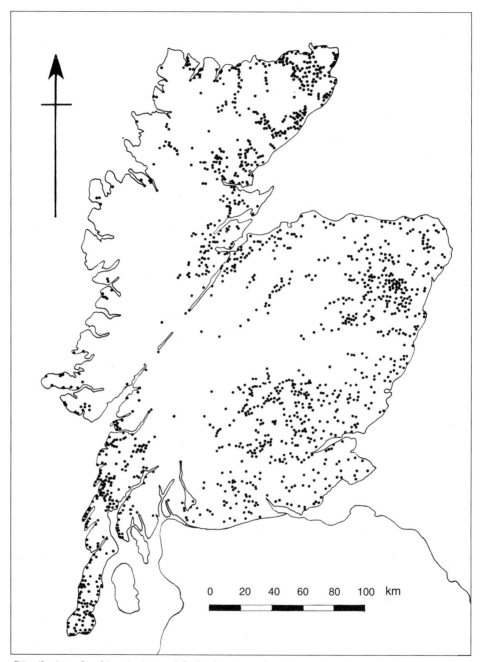

Distribution of prehistoric sites and finds of stone implements in mainland Scotland north of the Forth–Clyde line: a guide to the extent of human habitation at the beginning of the Pictish period.

desolate mountains' which, as Bede recorded,[1] separated the land of the northern Picts from that of the southern Picts.

Such is the pattern of prehistoric human activity in the land of the Picts; such the distribution of the population which gave rise to the Pictish nation. This is also the pattern recorded by the Picts themselves in the introduction to the *Pictish Chronicle*,[2] the earliest surviving version of which is a copy (in Latin) of an original document made during the reign of Kenneth son of Malcolm (971–95). Another copy of the same document was made about a hundred years later, in the reign of Malcolm son of Duncan, better known as Malcolm Canmore (1057–93).

'Cruithne son of Cinge, the father of the Picts inhabiting this island, reigned for 100 years. He had seven sons, whose names were Fib, Fidach, Fotlaig, Fortrenn, Cait, Ce and Circinn'.[3] These sons then reigned (apparently in succession, though this is not specifically stated) for a total of about 250 years. The later copy, which gives this introduction in Gaelic, adds the information that the seven sons of Cruithne divided the land into seven parts, 'as the poet relates':

> Seven sons of Cruithne then
> Into seven divided Alban,
> Cait, Ce, Cirig, a warlike clan,
> Fib, Fidach, Fotla, Fortrenn.

'And this was the name of each man of them and their territory.'[4] It also gives the family a pedigree extending back to Noah: 'Cruithne son of Cinge, son of Luctai, son of Partalan, son of Agnoin, son of Buain, son of Mais, son of Fathecht, son of Jafeth, son of Noe.' This is not history, but it is nonetheless of considerable interest. The names of the seven sons of Cruithne may not be the names of Pictish kings at all, but rather of seven provinces, or seven clans, which made up the Pictish kingdom. Some of these can be more or less easily identified.[5] Fib is Fife, and Cait Caithness. Fotlaig can be recognized in Atfodla, the old form of Atholl, and Mearns was formerly Maghcircin, the Plain of Circinn. Fortrenn is a district around Menteith and Strathearn, frequently mentioned in early sources. This leaves Ce and Fidach unplaced, and two important areas on the map, Aberdeenshire and the area around the Moray Firth, unmatched. It has been suggested that the name Ce may be seen in Bennachie, a mountain northwest of Aberdeen. This would leave Fidach to be linked with the Moray Firth area.

A later version of the story is to be found in a manuscript written in 1165, the first year of the reign of William brother of Malcolm (1165–1214), called William Rufus in the text, but better known as William the Lion. This land, we are told, was long ago divided by seven brothers into seven parts: Angus and Mearns, Atholl and Gowrie, Strathearn and Menteith, Fife and Fothreve, Marr and Buchan, Moray and Ross, and Caithness 'this side of the mountain and beyond the mountain, which mountain divides Caithness through the middle'.[6] There can be no doubt about the location of the seven divisions in this account.

A notable feature of the story is that, whichever version we read, there is no mention of the western part of the country, which during the historical period

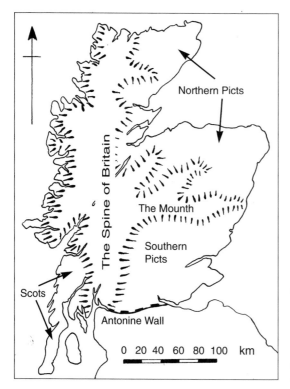

Northern Picts

The Spine of Britain

The Mounth

Southern
Picts

Scots

Antonine Wall

0 20 40 60 80 100   km

Sketch map (based on distribution map, p. 8) showing how the uninhabited highlands (the 'Spine of Britain' and the 'Mounth') separate the areas occupied by the Northern Picts, the Southern Picts, and the Scots from one another.

was occupied by the Dalriadan Scots. This strongly suggests that the Picts themselves saw their territory as comprising the whole of eastern Scotland, from the northern shores of Caithness right down to the Firth of Forth, but excluding the western coastal strip. This receives further support from the 1165 document, which, although it describes Argyll, in contemporary terms, as the western part of Scotland overlooking the Irish Sea, also refers to it as a distinct country, separated from Scotland by a range of mountains.[7]

If this story is not history, then what is it? Is it a myth or a legend and, if so, how did it start and when? Either it has some element of truth hidden in it, or someone, sometime, made it up.

One of the problems with interpreting this story is that during the two centuries from 975 to 1165 it was progressively modified. The most obvious change is the extension of the pedigree back to a biblical source. This is entirely in line with what was happening elsewhere in Britain. Thus the pedigree of Hywel Dda (Howel the Good), King of Wales (909–50), was traced back to Beli the Great, whose mother Anna was said to be 'the cousin of Mary the Virgin, mother of our Lord Jesus Christ'.[8] The ancestry of the kings of Wessex, as recorded in the *Anglo-Saxon Chronicle*, is traced back first to the Scandinavian god, Woden, and then, through him, to Noah and thence to Adam.[9] These pedigrees were not the result of careful analysis of records which have long since been lost or destroyed; they were propaganda, pure and simple, advertising the virtues of the ruling dynasty. The prime virtue of the dynasty of course was the fact that it was in power, but it was the responsibility of the agents of that dynasty (and in their interest too) to make sure that it remained in power; and this meant good advertising. Now effective advertising involves displaying the product in the best possible light rather than relaying the often quite mundane facts about it. And when, as in this story, that product was a dynasty and the nation over which it ruled had become Christian, it was felt that providing the dynasty with roots in the Bible was a promising line to pursue.

The other change is a little more subtle. In the 1165 version of the story the names of Fib, Fidach, Fotlaid, Fortrenn, Cait, Ce and Circin are no longer mentioned and the names of the districts over which they ruled have taken on a more modern form: Angus and Mearns, Atholl and Gowrie, Strathearn and Menteith, and so on. The eldest brother is the only one named, and he is called Angus, in keeping with the province over which he ruled. William the Lion ruled over the whole of Scotland, not by right of conquest but by descent from Kenneth mac Alpin and the Pictish dynasty which had ruled before him. Advertisements soon become dated and have to be changed or scrapped, and the 1165 version of our story is neither more nor less historical than the earlier versions; it is simply the same piece of propaganda brought up to date. What we do not know, and will probably never know, is how close the earliest surviving version of the story is to the original.

So what do we know? Clearly there can be little certainty about the names in the original story, but its importance lies less in the names of the brothers, or the clans that they represent, than in the fact that the whole thing was a piece of political propaganda. And, as such, it only makes sense in the context of the unification of a number (possibly seven) of formerly quite distinct tribes to form the Pictish nation. Whatever the means by which this union was achieved, whether by conquest or by treaty, it needed a new sense of national identity if it was to survive. This was provided by giving the tribes an origin in the sons of a common ancestor, Cruithne, the father of the Picts. And the story was given a poetic form in which it would have been recited or sung on great occasions and festivals, and thereby impressed on the memory of the people. The fiction would soon have become accepted as fact, and this 'fact' would then have become a significant element in giving the people a sense of their Pictish nationhood.

The other story about the origin of the Picts, the one told by Bede, seems to be Irish in origin rather than Pictish. Many Irish versions of this story have survived,[10] but they are all much later than Bede and likely to be far removed from the original. In most versions they came overland from Thrace, through Roman territory and then France, and eventually settled in Ireland. But they became too powerful there and were banished by Herimon who, with somewhat unlikely generosity, supplied them with the wives of the Irish warriors who had been drowned with their leader in the western sea. In another version, Cruithne, son of Cinge, went to the aid of the Britons of Fortren to fight against the Saxons. When they had won the battle and taken possession of the land, they suddenly discovered that they had no wives, because all the women of Alban (Scotland) had 'died of diseases', and this was the occasion for them to receive the women whose husbands had been drowned in the western sea. In the most colourful edition of this story, Cruithne then 'swore by the heaven and the earth, the sun and the moon, the sea and the land, the dew and the elements, that of women should be the royal succession among them for ever'.[11]

The essential core of this story, that the first Picts arrived without any women and had to beg wives from the Irish, remained unchanged for hundreds of years, and must have been familiar long before Bede reported it in 731. As a record of historical events it is neither very convincing nor very interesting, but as another piece of political propaganda it has greater possibilities. In Bede's version the story is presented as an explanation for the Pictish custom of succession through the female line, and this is also true of many of the later editions. It is not a very convincing explanation and is likely to have been thought up after the practice of matrilineal succession had become established, rather than being the actual origin of this custom. In a much later version it is used to explain the fact that the inhabitants of the Highlands spoke the Irish (Gaelic) language. And in another late version it was argued that since the succession was through the female line, and the wives of the first Picts had all been Irish, all the subsequent kings of the Picts were really Irish too! It was but a small step from this proposition to a belief that the Scots (coming from Ireland) had a perfect right to take over the whole kingdom for themselves.

These two stories, so very different in content and purpose, have just two things in common. First, Cruithne, the father of the Picts in the Pictish story, is also named in some versions of the Irish story. Second, it is implied in both stories that Britain is effectively divided into two parts, north and south. These two common factors should provide some clues to the actual situation at the time when the stories first began to circulate.

The name Cruithne, like that of his sons, is in reality the name of a people, the *Cruithni*. This is the Irish form of the Latin *Priteni* (or *Pritani*), as the inhabitants of Britain were called in late prehistoric times. It was not until the Roman period that this name was modified to the more familiar *Brittoni* (the Britons) for the people of the occupied (southern) part of Britain.[12] The Picts, far from being newcomers from Scythia, or Thrace as suggested in the Irish story, were in reality sons of Cruithne, natives of the land they occupied.

The seven sons of Cruithne, as we have seen, represent seven tribes or clans, whose territories all lie north of the Firth of Forth. In the Irish story the Picts settle in northern Britain because the south is already occupied by the Britons. This division of Britain into northern and southern parts makes little sense in late prehistoric times when, as Diodorus wrote, the island was thickly populated and held by 'many kings and potentates':[13] no suggestion here of a clear division into north and south. During the Roman period, however, the occupied zone became effectively a single political unit, a sort of pseudo-nation, with a rather well-defined northern boundary, either along Hadrian's Wall or along the Antonine Wall, which lies just south of the Firth of Forth.

These stories relate not to the origin of the Pictish peoples, but to the birth of the Pictish nation, a political and military unit which was far greater than the sum of its component parts. This birth took place sometime between the last quarter

The Antonine Wall (right) and ditch, the visible southern boundary of the Pictish kingdom for much of its history: view to the east near Rough Castle.

of the first century AD, when Agricola led the first Roman invasion of northern Britain, and the close of the third century, when the Picts were first mentioned by the Roman writer Eumenius. Agricola's most formidable opponents were the Caledonians, and these were just one among the dozen or so tribes shown as inhabiting northern Britain by the great second-century geographer, Ptolemy of Alexandria.[14]

CHAPTER 3

Pictish Chronology

The *Pictish Chronicle* is the most important source for the history of the Picts to
have survived. In order to make the best use of it, it is necessary to understand
what it is and, perhaps more importantly, what it is not. To start with, it is not a
chronicle, a record of events set against the year in which they occurred, like the
Anglo-Saxon Chronicle or the *Welsh Annals*. Indeed very few events are recorded
in the *Pictish Chronicle*. In essence, the *Pictish Chronicle* is a list of kings giving the
duration of each reign. It is exactly analogous to the Egyptian lists of kings and
pharaohs, whose dynasties provided a framework for eastern Mediterranean
chronology stretching back to 3000 BC; a chronology which was unrivalled until
the introduction of radiocarbon dating in the 1950s. Living in the twentieth
century AD, it is hard to imagine a time when the year we were living in did not
have a number attached to it, a time when the new year was not automatically
accompanied by a change in that number. From the registration of our births, the
events of our lives are recorded in terms of dates which are international in their
application. It was not always so, and it was not so for the Picts. For them, as for
the ancient Egyptians, the best available chronology was provided by the ruling
dynasty itself. The few dated events recorded in the *Pictish Chronicle* are given in
the following form:

> Bridei son of Mailcon reigned for 30 years. In the eighth year of his reign he
> was baptised by Saint Columba.[1]
>
> Kenneth son of Alpin, the first of the Scots, ruled fruitfully over Pictavia for
> 16 years . . . In the seventh year of his reign he transported the relics of Saint
> Columba to the church he had built, and invaded Saxonia [Lothian] six times;
> and burnt Dunbar to the ground, and took possession of Melrose.[2]

This system of dating was in common use throughout the Middle Ages and
was easy to maintain by a regular celebration of the anniversary of the King's
accession. Even now, the Queen's official birthday, on or near the anniversary of
her coronation, is a date to be remembered, when gifts in the form of coveted
honours are bestowed on favoured ministers of state, civil servants, officers in the
armed forces, and other citizens. Such a system is perfectly satisfactory so long as
the reference dynasty remains stable. To find out how long ago a particular event
happened, all you needed to do was add up the lengths of the intervening reigns.
The familiar AD dates, pioneered in Britain by Bede in the early eighth century

and followed by King Alfred in the second half of the ninth century, did not come into general use until much later.

So the *Pictish Chronicle* is a chronology rather than a chronicle in the true sense. Since chronology is absolutely fundamental to any sensible approach to history, we must give this chronology our careful consideration. William Skene, in his monumental volume of chronicles of the Picts and Scots published in 1867, printed seven versions of the *Pictish Chronicle*.[3] The earliest of these have already been referred to in the last chapter, the first dated 971–95 and the second, of which two copies are printed by Skene, dated 1040–72. The four remaining versions were dated by Skene at 1187, 1251, 1280 and 1317.[4] It should not be supposed, however, that the surviving manuscripts are as old as these dates would suggest. Far from it. The 971–95 version, for example, only survives in a fourteenth-century copy; and the 1251 version in a copy made about 1708, of a copy made before 1660, of a document (now lost) from the register of the Priory of St Andrews.[5]

The texts of these several versions of the *Pictish Chronicle* differ from one another, to a greater or lesser extent, for a variety of reasons. First there are scribal errors: simple copying errors, mistakes due to the difficulty of reading illegible or archaic handwriting, and mistakes due to the difficulty of understanding documents written in an unfamiliar language. These are human errors analogous to modern printing and editorial errors, but whereas modern books are printed in their thousands and any errors therefore reproduced exactly in every copy of a particular edition, each manuscript of an early text is an individual product with its own peculiar errors, though perhaps also faithfully reproducing the errors of earlier scribes in the chain leading back to the original text. There may also be intentional deviations from the text being copied, either addition of new material thought to be of interest or omission of details not considered relevant to the purpose for which the copy is being made. This sounds like a pretty unpromising start, but it is not as bad as it seems. It is perfectly possible, by careful comparison of the different versions of the *Pictish Chronicle*, to detect scribal errors and, to some extent, to recognize the intentional addition or omission of material. Let us begin by looking at one early Pictish king and the length of his reign. The versions are numbered in date order, with the two copies of the 1140–72 version being numbered 2a and 2b.

1	Necton morbet filius Erip	24 years
2a	Nectan morbrec mac Erip	24 years
2b	Nectan mor breac mac Eirip	24 years
3	Nethan chelemot	10 years
4	Netthan thelchamoth	10 years
5	Nectane Celtaniech	10 years
6	Nectan celchamoch	10 years

Clearly we can no longer be sure whether the king's name should be spelt Necton, Nectan, Nectane, Nethan or Netthan (standard spelling: Nechtan[6]), but this is of relatively little importance historically. Much more interesting is the fact that, as far as this king is concerned, the surviving manuscripts of the *Pictish Chronicle* fall into two groups: in one he is identified as the son of Erip and reigned for 24 years, and in the other he only reigned for 10 years. If we try the same test on other kings, we get similar results, for example:

1	Unuist filius Wrguist	12 years
2a	Uidnuist filius Uurguist	12 years
2b	Uidnuist filius Uurgust	12 years
3	Hungus filius Fergusane	9 years
4	Hungus filius Fergusa	10 years
5	Hungus fitz Fergusa	10 years
6	Hungus filius Fergus	10 years

If we look at the few snippets of historical information given in the *Pictish Chronicle*, we find the same grouping, for example the passage relating to the baptism of Bridei son of Mailcon (Brude son of Maelchon):

1	In octavo anno regni ejus baptizatus est sancto a Columba.
2a	In octavo anno regni eius baptizatus est a sancto Columba.
2b	In ochtaauuo anno regni eit baibtizatus est e Sancto Columba.
3	Istum convertit Sanctus Columba ad fidem.
4	Hunc ad fidem convertit Sanctus Columba.
5	Saint Columbe et Palladius conuerterunt cesti a la foy Cristien.
6	Hunc conuertit Sanctus Columba.

The same essential information is given in each version, except for the fact that the 1280 version adds the name of St Palladius. The information is the same, but the text falls into the same two groups as before. In the first, the exact year is given and the king is 'baptized by St Columba', whereas in the second 'St Columba converted' him.

These, together with many other similar examples, make it quite clear that the surviving manuscripts of the *Pictish Chronicle* belong to two groups – group A (971–95, 1040–72) and group B (1187, 1251, 1280, 1317) – which are ultimately derived from two different manuscript originals, each compiled some time after the arrival of St Columba. This fact, which has been known for well over a hundred years,[7] is of the greatest importance. It means that instead of having to study seven lists scattered through the pages of Skene's volume, it should be possible to recognize and eliminate many of the scribal errors, together with intentional additions and omissions, and reduce these to two master lists of the Pictish kings and their reigns. These can then be arranged side by side and the genuine differences between them analysed for historical significance. Two such lists, for the kings from Gede to Kenneth mac Alpin, are assembled in Appendix 1. Earlier kings, who only appear in group A manuscripts, have been omitted and all supplementary historical notes excluded, whether or not they may be original.

The lists are printed next to each other for ease of comparison. The reigns are

Left: eleventh-century round tower at Abernethy (Irish architectural influence). The group A version of the Pictish Chronicle was still being kept up to date at Abernethy when this tower was built.

Right: late tenth early solidus eleventh-century round tower at Brechin (Irish architectural influence). The 'Brechin Chronicle', incorporating a copy of the group A version of the Pictish Chronicle, was written at about the time this tower was built.

numbered from 1 (Gud or Gede) to 79 (Kinadius or Kinart son of Alpin). Kings who appear in both lists have been given the same number and will be found in the same position on opposite pages. Kings who appear in one list only have also been given a number, but this is represented by a gap in the opposite list. These gaps are artificial (each list taken by itself being continuous), but serve to highlight the periods of difference between the two lists.

In the earliest period, from Gud to Wradech (Feradach) uecla (1 to 21), the group A manuscripts contain a much fuller record than those of group B. In this part of the record there can be little doubt that both lists were drawing on oral tradition, and the differences reflect differential recall of that tradition. The many points they have in common, however, are an indication that both groups share the same tradition.

In the middle period, from Feradach uecla to Nechtan son of Derile (21 to 51), the lists correspond very closely. After the reign of Nechtan, however, the differences between the two master lists become so great that they cannot possibly be attributed to scribal error. It follows that the two groups of manuscripts are ultimately derived from king lists maintained in two distinct centres (probably churches) which, during periods of intermittent civil war, came under the rule of different kings. The reigns of the kings in these two lists should of course add up to the same total number of years, each of the lists thus providing an equally valid basis for a Pictish chronology. This, unfortunately, is not the case.

The best known chronological difference between the two master lists occurs immediately before the reign of Kenneth mac Alpin. In the group A lists the three kings immediately preceding Kenneth are Uven (Eoganan) son of Oengus (3 years), Wrad (Ferat) son of Bargoit (3 years) and Bred (1 year). In the group B lists three more kings are interpolated between Bred and Kenneth mac Alpin: Kenneth son of Ferat (1 year), Brude son of Fokel (2 years) and Drust son of Ferat (3 years). These three extra kings have been referred to as local kings[8] and as resistance leaders making a last stand against Kenneth mac Alpin.[9] Either way, it would seem that Kenneth did not become king of all the Picts at once, and in the source area for the group B manuscripts his rule was resisted for a total of 6 years. And yet in all the lists Kenneth's reign is given as 16 years. This may be compared with a much more familiar example. James VI, son of Mary Queen of Scots, was proclaimed King of Scotland in July 1567, when he was just a year old. In the thirty-sixth year of his reign, in March 1603, he became King of England, following the death of his first cousin, Queen Elizabeth. He died on 27 March 1625. How long did he reign? The answer to this question depends on whether you are Scottish, and talking of the reign of James VI, or English, and referring to the reign of James I. The royal clerks of this period were fairly careful in such matters and, on the relatively rare occasions when they did not use dates AD, they used such phrases as 'in the third year of our reign of England'.

The period of greatest difference between the two master lists, from the reign of Nechtan son of Derile to that of Constantine son of Wrguist (Fergus), is also the period of greatest disagreement between the different manuscripts comprising group B. Of the four versions printed by Skene, the 1187 copy seems to be distinctly lacking in detail for this period, and the 1280 copy is generally the least

Late eleventh/early twelfth-century St Rule's Tower (English architectural influence) at St Andrews. The group B version of the Pictish Chronicle *was still being written up (possibly at St Andrews) long after this tower was built.*

reliable. A comparison of the 1251 and 1317 copies shows how difficult it is to interpret the king lists of this period. Two features of these lists seem worthy of special note. The first is the number of returns of the same king after a period of 'absence': Nechtan son of Derile (or Decili) and Oengus son of Brude, for example. Of Oengus son of Brude, the 1251 copy says he reigned for 6 months and again for 36 years, without stating when the second reign appeared in the sequence. The 1317 copy gives both reigns their place in the sequence, and makes it clear that the 36 year reign was the second reign of the same king. The 1280 copy applies this information to a different king, Alpin son of Feradech, and says that he reigned for 6 months at one time, was expelled, but afterwards reigned for 30 years. The second point of interest is the number of very short reigns: 6 months, 9 months and 1 year. In the lists which follow, 'f' stands for 'filius' (son).

1251 king list		1317 king list	
Brude f Decili	31 years	Brude f Decili	31 years
Ferthen his brother	18 years	Nectan his brother	18 years
Garnath f Ferath	24 years	Garnach f Ferach	24 years
Oengusu f Ferguse	16 years	Oengusa f Fergus	16 years
Netthan f Decili	9 months	Nectan f Derili	9 months

1251 king list		1317 king list	
Alpin f Feret	6 months		
Onegussa f Brude	6 months	Oengus f Brude	6 months
Brude f Tonegus	8 years	Alpinus f Engus	8 years
Durst f Talorgen	1 year	Drust f Talargan	5 years
		Hungus f Fergus	10 years
Engus f Brude	36 years	Engus f Brude	36 years
		Brude f Engus	2 years
		Alpin f Engus	8 years
		Drust f Talargan	1 year
Talargan f Drustan	4 years	Talargan f Drustan	4 years
Talargan f Tenegus	5 years	Talargan f Engus	5 years
Constantinus f Fergusa	42 years	Constantinus f Fergus	42 years
Hungus f Fergusa	10 years	Hungus f Fergus	10 years

Some of the differences between the two lists shown above (and the other two in group B) may be due to ordinary scribal errors in copying from the original. But the fact that the copies are in complete harmony at the beginning and end of the sequence suggests that another factor is involved. The probability is that the originals were difficult to interpret because the contemporary situation had been so complex that the original 'chroniclers' had found it almost beyond their power to express the rapidly changing succession of kings in a simple form. It was pointed out earlier in this chapter that using the succession of kings as a guide to the passage of time works very well so long as the dynasty remains stable. What we are seeing in the period discussed above is a breakdown of that required stability.

To find a well-known historical analogy for this period, we may refer to the period of English history known as the Wars of the Roses. The succession of kings during this time may be expressed in Pictish king list form as follows:

Henry son of Henry (Henry VI)	38½ years
Edward son of Richard (Edward IV)	10½ years
Henry son of Henry (Henry VI)	6 months
Edward son of Richard (Edward IV)	2 years
Edward son of Edward (Edward V)	3 months
Richard son of Richard (Richard III)	2 years
Henry son of Edmund (Henry VII)	23½ years

This sequence is simpler than the Pictish situation in one respect, namely that when there was a change of king it affected the whole country. In other respects it is very similar to the Pictish list, in particular repeated reigns of the same king (Henry VI and Edward IV) and very short reigns (3 months, 6 months and 2 years). Of particular interest from a chronological point of view is the second reign of Henry VI. He dated this brief return as the forty-ninth year from the beginning of his reign and the first of his restoration to royal power. How many

Pictish kings (or their chroniclers) would have concerned themselves with the second part of this statement?

The fortunes of the kings in this period of English history are well known. Henry VI, after several years as a fugitive, was captured in 1465 and imprisoned in the Tower of London till 1470. He was captured again in 1471, after the Battle of Barnet, and returned to the Tower. Later that year he was murdered, after his only son, Edward Prince of Wales, had been killed at the Battle of Tewkesbury. Edward V and his younger brother, Richard, the 'Princes in the Tower', were imprisoned and also possibly murdered in the Tower. Richard III was slain at the Battle of Bosworth. It may well be surmised that the lives of the Pictish kings in the period we have been considering were also punctuated by battles and periods of imprisonment.

But what was that period of Pictish history? What were the dates of the kings who fought those long-forgotten battles, and lost and regained their kingdoms? That is just the sort of information that the *Pictish Chronicle* should be able to supply but, since the different versions give timescales which differ by as much as fifty years in a period of less than two hundred, this is just what it cannot do until it has been calibrated with the aid of independent dating evidence.

Kenneth mac Alpin died 'in the Ides of February, on the third day of the week'. This statement, in the earliest 971–95 copy of the *Pictish Chronicle*, enables the year of his death to be identified as 860.[10] Two earlier markers are provided by Bede. First, he recorded the arrival of St Columba in the year 564, 'in the ninth year of the reign of the powerful Pictish king, Bride son of Meilochon'.[11] Second, he gives a detailed account of the correspondence between Ceolfrid, Abbot of Wearmouth, and Nechtan, King of the Picts, regarding the observance of Easter. This correspondence he dated to the year 710,[12] and Nechtan can only be Nechtan son of Derile, after whose (first) reign the period of civil war began. The most detailed evidence for testing the different versions of the *Pictish Chronicle* is provided by Irish sources, the most important of which are the *Annals of Ulster* and the *Annals of Tigernach*,[13] and these will be considered in the next chapter.

CHAPTER 4

Dates from Ireland

The arrival of St Columba in Scotland, the founding of his abbey on Iona and the conversion of Brude son of Mailchon brought the Picts into the sphere of interest of the Irish annalists. Their records survive in the annals written by Tigernach of Clonmacnoise, who died in 1088, and in the *Annals of Ulster*, compiled by Senait mac Manus in 1498. These annals in their original manuscript form did not have dated (AD) years, but these have been supplied (with varying success) by subsequent editors. The dates used in this chapter are those given by Skene.[1]

According to these Irish annals, St Columba sailed from Ireland in 563 in his forty-second year. The same annals record the death of Brude son of Maelchon, King of the Picts, in 584. The time interval between these two events might appear at first sight to be 21 years, but could in fact be anything between just over 20 (if Columba arrived late in 563 and Brude died early in 584) and almost 22 years (if Columba arrived early in 563 and Brude died late in 584). In all versions of the *Pictish Chronicle*, Brude son of Maelchon reigned for 30 years and was converted by St Columba in the eighth year of his reign. We do not know whether he reigned for 30 years to the nearest whole number, whether he died in the thirtieth year of his reign or whether he died after having reigned for 30 whole years. The time interval between his conversion and his death might be anything between less than 21 (if he was converted late in the eighth year of his reign and died before he had reigned for 30 full years) or nearly 23 years (if he was converted early in the eighth year of his reign and died well on in his thirty-first year). There is also the unknown time which Columba would have required to plan and carry out his expedition up the Great Glen to meet Brude at his palace somewhere near Inverness.

The dates in the Irish annals are consistent with the statements contained in the *Pictish Chronicle*. They are equally consistent with Bede's statement that Brude was converted in the ninth year of his reign. To use the dates given in the *Annals of Tigernach* and the *Annals of Ulster* to test the chronologies given in the different versions of the *Pictish Chronicle*, it must first be established that the Pictish and Irish records are independent of one another.

The next three kings in the Pictish lists are Gartnait son of Domnach, who reigned for 11 years (20 in the group B lists), Nechtan nephew or grandson of Uerb, who reigned for 20 years (21 in the group B lists), and Cinioch son of Lutrin, who reigned for 19 years (14 or 24 in the group B lists). Adding these reign lengths to the date of Brude's death, we get approximate dates for the deaths of these kings as 595 (or 604) for Gartnait, 615 (or 625) for Nechtan and 634 (639 or 649) for Cinioch. According to the *Annals of Tigernach*, Gartnaidh, King of the Picts, died in 599. The death of Nechtan passed without comment by the Irish annalists, unless he is the Nechtan mac Canand who died in 621; but there is nothing to suggest that this Nechtan was a king. Cinaetha mac Luchtren, King of the Picts, is recorded as having died in 631. The lack of correspondence of the dates, together with the non-appearance of Nechtan nephew or grandson of Uerb in the Irish annals, is a clear indication that the Pictish and Irish records are independent of one another. Neither could have been derived from the other.

For the next 75 years, the agreement between the Pictish Chronicle and the Irish annals is excellent, right up to 706, when Nechtan son of Derelei came to the throne and the period of civil war discussed in the last chapter began. Even before the time of Nechtan, trouble may have been brewing. The Irish annals record that Drust son of Domhnaill was expelled from his kingdom in 672 and died in 678; and that Tarachin (Tarain) was similarly treated in 697 and fled to Ireland in 699. For the next period the group A and group B versions of the *Pictish Chronicle* are very different.

Taking the date of Brude's death as 584 and adding the successive reign lengths, a detailed comparison can be made between the Pictish and Irish chronologies (Appendix 2). The correlation between the earliest version of the *Pictish Chronicle* and the dates recorded in the Irish annals is remarkable. Over a period of three hundred years the difference between the Pictish and Irish dates is never greater than 4 years either way. As a guide to chronology, this version of the *Pictish Chronicle* is thus demonstrated to be thoroughly reliable back to the middle of the sixth century. In spite of this it is widely believed that all earlier parts of the list belong 'to the mists of legend and antiquarian invention'.[2]

Before going on to discuss the earlier chronology, we should see how a group B list stands up to the Irish test. The 1317 copy of the group B Pictish version of the chronicle (Appendix 2) shows a very poor correlation with the dates provided by the Irish annals. At the end of the same three hundred year period the Pictish dates are in error by over a hundred years. Furthermore, throughout the whole period the errors are in the same direction. The timescale indicated by this list is consistently too long. For one reason or another, many of the reign lengths must have been overestimated; others may have been duplicated. Also, particularly in the later part of the list, many of the kings seem to have died unnoticed by the Irish annalists. The list is not without historical interest but, as a guide to chronology, it is worse than useless.

Having established that the earliest (970–95) version of the *Pictish Chronicle* provides a reliable timescale for the three centuries from the arrival of St Columba to the death of Kenneth mac Alpin, let us now turn our attention to the earlier kings. At first sight they look perfectly acceptable for about a century before the reign of Brude son of Maelchon; but then we come to Drust son of Erp, who 'reigned for a hundred years and fought a hundred battles'. Here we have a legendary hero, a hero of such renown moreover that this brief notice of his career appears in every version of the *Pictish Chronicle*. Before Drust son of Erp, history and legend are intermingled to such an extent that any meaningful chronology is quite out of the question. The list of kings from Drust son of Erp to Brude son of Maelchon is given below, with dates worked back from Brude's death in 584.

971–95 king list	reign	dates
Drust son of Erp	100 years	
Talore son of Aniel	4 years	452–6
Necton son of Erip	24 years	456–80
Drest Gurthinmoch	30 years	480–510
Galanan erilich	12 years	510–22
Drest son of Gyrom and		
Drest son of Wdrost together	5 years	522–7
Drest son of Girom alone	5 years	527–32
Garthnach son of Girom	7 years	532–9
Cailtram son of Girom	1 year	539–40
Talorg son of Muircholaich	11 years	540–51
Drest son of Munait	1 year	551–2
Galam cennaleph alone	1 year	552–3
with Brude	1 year	553–4
Brude son of Maelchon	30 years	554–84

The only date recorded by the Irish annalists for this earlier period is the death of Brude's predecessor, Galam cennaleph ('Cendaeladh king of the Picts' in the *Annals of Tigernach* and 'Cennalat king of the Picts' in the *Annals of Ulster*) in 580. But comparison with the dates deduced from the *Pictish Chronicle* suggests that this date is 26 years too late. A sudden error of 26 years in a record which had been accurate to within 4 years for three centuries seems highly improbable and requires an explanation, though it does, incidentally, add weight to the conclusion, reached above, that these are quite independent sources for the history of the period.

Three possible reasons for the discrepancy suggest themselves:

1   the reign of Brude lasted only 4 years, and not 30 as given in the chronicle;
2   the identity of Galam cennaleph with the king whose death is recorded in the Irish annals is mistaken;
3   Brude may not have been ruling over the whole Pictish nation for all of his 30 year reign.

If Brude's reign really only lasted for 4 years, the statement about his conversion by St Columba in the eighth year of his reign, which is found in every version of the *Pictish Chronicle*, becomes meaningless. Furthermore the account of Brude's reign and conversion are consistent with details recorded by Bede[3] over two hundred years before the earliest surviving version of the chronicle was first copied.

Galam cennaleph is called Tagalad, Tagaled and Tagalach in the group B versions of the *Pictish Chronicle*. It is possible that his identification with the Cendaeladh or Cennalat of the Irish annals is mistaken, but this is no more than a possibility.

It should certainly not be assumed that all of the kings whose reigns are listed in the *Pictish Chronicle* ruled over the whole united Pictish nation. We have already seen evidence in the last chapter, from the differences between the group A and group B versions of the chronicle, that there was a period of civil war in the eighth and ninth centuries, during which the kingdom was at times partitioned. This is supported by a passage found only in the earliest (971–95) copy of the chronicle, where Nechtan son of Erip is described as 'Nechtan the Great, king of all the provinces of the Picts'.[4] This clearly implies that some of his predecessors or successors did not have such universal authority.

Let us suppose that Brude really did reign for 30 years, and that his predecessor, Galam cennaleph, is correctly identified with the Cendaeladh or Cennalat, King of the Picts, who died in 580. These two assumptions can only be reconciled if Brude's reign is divided into two periods: a longer early period in which he ruled only over part of the kingdom, and a shorter later period during which he was indeed King of all the Picts. This is most simply illustrated by means of a table, in which the kingdom is for a period of about 26 years, divided into two parts (A and B) without, at this stage, any implication as to their geographical location.

King of part A	King of all Picts	King of part B
	Drust son of Erp	
	Talore son of Aniel (478–82)	
	Nechtan son of Erip (482–506)	
	Drest Gurthinmoch (506–36)	
	Galanan erilich (536–48)	
	Drust son of Gyrom with Drust son of Wdrost (548–53)	
Drust son of Girom (553–8)		
Garthnait son of Girom (558–65)		
Cailtram son of Girom (565–6)		Brude son of Maelchon
Talorg son of Muircholaich (566–77)		(554–79)
Drust son of Munait (577–8)		
Calam cennaleph (578–9)		
	Galam cennaleph with Brude son of Maelchon (579–80)	
	Brude son of Maelchon (580–4)	

According to this explanation, after the death of Drust son of Wdrost, Drust son of Girom failed to hold the kingdom together. Brude son of Maelchon was chosen to rule the breakaway part (part B). After outliving several kings of part A, he eventually made an alliance with Galam cennaleph, ruled jointly with him for a year, and then, after his death, ruled over the whole kingdom for a further 4 years. The date for the beginning of Brude's reign agrees within a year with the end of the joint rule of Drust son of Girom and Drust son of Wdrost. This is consistent with the accuracy we have come to expect of this copy of the *Pictish Chronicle*.

The Kirk of St Bride, Abernethy, taking the Pictish Chronicle dating quite literally, records its dedication in AD 457. It is more likely to have been founded 27 years later, in AD 484.

This scheme has the effect of adding 27 years to all of the estimated dates before the death of Brude. Thus the reign of Nechtan son of Erip would have begun in 482 rather than 455. The importance of this lies in the statement in the *Pictish Chronicle*[5] that, in the third year of Nechtan's reign, Darlugdach Abbess of Kildare left Ireland on a mission to 'Britain'. In the second year of her mission, Nechtan met her and presented her with land at Abernethy for the foundation of a church. Darlugdach died in about 526, some 40 years after the commencement of her mission according to the suggested chronology. It is much less likely (though not quite impossible) that she set off from Ireland in 458, about 68 years before her death. She would have been a very young missionary (say 22 years old) *and* had an exceptionally long life (say 90 years).

The balance of evidence is strongly in favour of a divided Pictish kingdom during most of the reign of Brude son of Maelchon. The discussion so far has been quite intentionally limited to chronological considerations. The historical implications will be considered in Chapter 11.

CHAPTER 5

The United Kingdom of the Picts

We have seen evidence in the last two chapters for divisions in the kingdom of the Picts; around the middle of the sixth century and again through much of the eighth and into the ninth century. But this only serves to emphasize the fact that to the outside world, whether Roman or British, English or Irish, the Picts were viewed as a single nation. Indeed, from the evidence of the *Pictish Chronicle* it is clear that the Picts saw themselves in the same light. The united Pictish nation was the norm. The periods of disunity were breaks from that normality. This great achievement of the Picts, for it was nothing less, stands in impressive contrast to the contemporary history of the other nations of Britain.

When they emerged from the wreckage of the Roman occupation, the Britons were a nation only in their common language and Christian religion, and in their more or less superficial Romano-British culture. By the middle of the fifth century the English (Saxons) had become a serious menace in the southern and eastern parts of Britain. For a time the Britons presented a united front against them, under the inspired leadership of Ambrosius Aurelianus, culminating in the great victory at Mount Badon, in about 500. But Ambrosius was not a king and Britain, far from being a kingdom, was a loose and transient confederation of tribes, much as it had been 450 years earlier, at the time of the Roman invasion. The opportunity presented by the peace which followed Badon was squandered. Instead of consolidating the unity forged in the face of the enemy, the kings of the Britons fell to civil strife, each trying to gain power at the expense of his neighbours and all thereby incurring the wrath of Gildas the priest.[1]

At no time was there a king of all the provinces of the Britons, a British equivalent of the Pictish kings. Kings there were in plenty, and we know their names and their genealogies, but they were kings of Gwynedd, of Powys, of Dyfed and, beyond the confines of Wales, of Dumnonia (Devon and Cornwall) and Strathclyde. Indeed the very idea of a British kingdom, as distinct from its component parts, seems to have surfaced for the first time in Geoffrey of Monmouth's history,[2] written early in the twelfth century. In this work, Ambrosius is portrayed as King of Britain, and is followed, a generation later, by his nephew King Arthur. Geoffrey was not so much falsifying the history of Dark Age Britain as putting it into a medieval form which would have been acceptable to his readers. King Arthur has even less historical validity in this period than King Ambrosius.[3] In the real history of post-Roman Britain, division was the norm and unity the rarest exception; and this remained true in Wales right up to the time of its conquest by Edward I.

The English, like the British, had many kings, ruling over such people as the Angles of Mercia and Northumbria, the East Angles, the East Saxons, the South Saxons, the West Saxons and the Kentish folk; people whose names are still imprinted on the map of England. From the end of the fifth century, all the kings south of the Humber acknowledged (from time to time) the overlordship of one king, who was known as the *Bretwalda* (Britain ruler).[4] The first of these was Aelle, King of the South Saxons (probably late fifth century), and he was followed by Ceaulin, King of the West Saxons (mid-sixth century), Ethelbert, King of the Kentish folk, and Redwald, King of the East Saxons. From then on it was a struggle for supremacy. Redwald was followed by three Northumbrian kings; then Northumbria gave way to the growing power of Mercia. By the end of the eighth century, Offa (757–96), the greatest of the Mercian kings, could justifiably style himself King of the English. Meanwhile, the power of Wessex was rising, and a hundred years later the Wessex dynasty of the kings of England was firmly established by Alfred the Great (871–99). The kingdom of England, as a political unit, thus developed gradually over a period of some four hundred years.

The Scottish kingdom of Dalriada was the smallest of the four nations of Britain listed by Bede. As a kingdom it is comparable less with the other three nations than with the smaller kingdoms of which they were composed: with Gwynedd or Powys, for example, or East Anglia or Wessex, or Fortrenn or Atholl. The apparent success of the Picts in achieving political unity should therefore be compared with the struggles of the English and the failure of the British to reach that state. What were the conditions which favoured the development of the Pictish nation, or did the Picts have some special political skill, which the others failed either to recognize or to apply?

Among the conditions which led to the development of the Pictish nation, we have to admit a substantial element of luck. The first Roman invasion of northern Britain began in AD 79 and continued for 6 years under the inspired leadership of Agricola, the Governor of Britain.[5] Agricola's campaigns culminated in the crushing defeat of a large Caledonian army at Mons Graupius, probably somewhere north of Aberdeen, in 84. His advance was accompanied by the construction of roads and the building of forts at strategic points, and by the end of 84 he had the whole country south of the Moray Firth under his control. It was at this point that the Emperor Domitian chose to recall him. At about the same time, reinforcements were urgently needed elsewhere on the frontiers of the empire, in Germany and along the Danube, and this necessitated a reduction in the strength of the Roman army stationed in Britain. Far from completing the conquest of northern Britain, it soon became apparent that the territorial gains made by Agricola could not be maintained. In less than 10 years the Roman occupation of Caledonia (the name used by Tacitus for the country north of the Firth of Forth) was at an end. Having failed to conquer the whole of Britain, the Romans were forced to establish a frontier zone between Roman Britain to the south and Caledonia to the north. Two great barriers were constructed in the first half of the second century: first Hadrian's Wall, stretching from the Solway Firth in the west to the estuary of the Tyne in the east; then, further north, the Antonine Wall, crossing the narrower isthmus between the Forth and the Clyde. The people of Caledonia were left in peace to learn from their experience.

It is difficult to plot the progress of the tribes of Caledonia towards Pictish nationhood because we do not really know the tribal geography of the country at any one time. The classical writers, who are our only source of information, seldom provide sufficient detail. The great second-century Greek geographer, Ptolemy, mentions four tribes inhabiting the country between the Firth of Forth and the Moray Firth: the *Caledonii*, *Vacomagi*, *Taezali* and *Venicones*. Tacitus, in his account of Agricola's campaign, mentions none of these. He refers generally to the 'tribes of Caledonia' without naming them, and calls all the people Britons, regardless of their tribal affiliations. The only Caledonian tribe he names is the *Boresti*, from whom Agricola took hostages after the battle of Mons Graupius.[6]

The concept of a multitribal national identity in Caledonia probably had its origin in the formation of military alliances. The first of these, in the final season of Agricola's invasion, is recorded by Tacitus. The Britons of Caledonia, realizing what they were up against, formed an alliance and 'ratified the confederacy of their tribes by conference and sacrifice'.[7] But when it came to a pitched battle they were unable to match the superior armour and tactics of the Romans, in spite of the advantages of high ground and greater numbers. But a start had been made.

Towards the end of the second century the tribes of Caledonia were once again at war with the Romans, but this time they themselves were the aggressors. In about the year 181 they swarmed across the Antonine Wall, attacked a Roman army and slew a general, and it was several years before peace could be restored.[8] Then in 196 the Governor of Britain, Clodius Albinus, crossed over into Gaul with a large army in a vain attempt to have himself proclaimed emperor. With the garrison of Hadrian's Wall thereby seriously depleted, the northern tribes attacked again. Dio Cassius, in his contemporary account of this war,[9] wrote that there were 'two principal races of the Britons, the Caledonians and the *Maeatae*, and the names of the others have been merged in these two'. Of these two 'super-tribes', the *Maeatae* lived close to the wall, and the Caledonians beyond them to the north.

If Dio Cassius is to be taken literally, the *Maeatae* and the Caledonians represent something more than a mere military alliance of their component tribes, created to meet a specific challenge, only to be dissolved again when that situation had passed. He spoke of them as two principal and quite distinct races and implied that there was a military alliance between them. Whatever the precise interpretation of Dio's statement, it is quite clear that the *Maeatae* and the Caledonians presented a very formidable challenge to the security of Roman Britain. Unable to gain a military victory over the *Maeatae*, the Roman Governor, Virius Lupus, was forced to buy them off with a large sum of money.[10] In 208 the Emperor Severus arrived in Britain with large reinforcements but, in spite of the most serious Roman invasion since the time of Agricola, the *Maeatae* and Caledonians were still putting up a solid resistance when Severus died in 211.

War broke out again before the end of the third century and culminated in another Roman invasion, this time under the Emperor Constantius in 306. Like Severus before him, Constantius died in York after his campaign in the north. From this time onwards Roman writers referred to the Britons north of the walls as Picts. Sometimes they mentioned subsidiary tribal units, in such phrases as 'Caledonians and other Picts' or, referring to an invasion from the north in 367, 'Picts divided into two peoples, *Dicalydones* and *Verturiones*'; but generally they just spoke of Picts, without any qualification.[11] The Pictish nation had arrived. The tribal units within the Pictish nation were still there, just as they were in the eighth century when we read in the *Annals of Ulster* of Talorgan son of Drostan king of Atholl or Brude king of Fortren.[12] The Pictish nation was something new and different, something greater than the sum of its component parts, and it was destined to last for more than five hundred years.

There is no evidence to suggest that the tribes of Caledonia were any more peaceable than those of southern Britain in the pre-Roman Iron Age. Among the most familiar archeological sites in southern Britain are the Iron Age hillforts. Though some of these, such as Maiden Castle in Dorset, were certainly defended against the Roman invaders,[13] it is quite clear that they were not built as a line of defence against an external enemy. They became necessary because of intertribal warfare. In Scotland the evidence for such warfare is no less compelling. Hillforts, including the well-known vitrified forts, are widespread except in the far north, in Caithness and Sutherland, where their place is taken by those remarkable drystone castles known as brochs.

Fort or broch, tribe or farmstead, south or north, the need for defence was universal, and the vast amount of labour expended on these works implies a very real threat of attack. The growth of the Pictish nation was not facilitated by an unusually harmonious and peaceful background in the pre-Roman Iron Age. Such a background, quite apart from being incompatible with the archeological evidence, would hardly have given rise to the fiercest adversaries that the Romans were to meet anywhere in Britain.

Without obvious natural advantages, either of background or of circumstance, the Pictish kingdom came of age in a period of about two hundred years from the first Roman invasion. It took the kings of Wessex more than twice that time to establish their supremacy among the English kings and to attain general recognition as kings of England. The Welsh, the last remnant of the British tribes and a much closer analogy to the Picts, had their territory marked out by Offa, King of Mercia (757–96). Offa's Dyke defined a boundary between the estuaries of the Severn and the Dee, just as the Antonine Wall had defined a boundary between the Forth and the Clyde. The country to the west of the dyke was Welsh and that to the east was English; but there the similarity ended. The tribes beyond the Antonine Wall combined to form the Pictish nation. Those beyond Offa's Dyke failed to form a united Welsh kingdom, and five hundred years later they paid the price for their disunity when they were conquered by Edward I of England.

History does not reveal just how the Picts succeeded in creating a single united kingdom out of the warlike tribes of Caledonia. It does, however, tell us how the Welsh failed to achieve such a union, and this may provide a clue.

CHAPTER 6

The Female Royal Line

The Pictish achievement was the conversion of a series of military alliances into a united kingdom. A military alliance is a temporary expedient and does not affect the sovereignty of the tribes involved, particularly if its leader is not himself a king. In post-Roman Britain, Ambrosius Aurelianus was such a leader. He founded no ruling dynasty, and when he died the alliance he had led so effectively against the Saxons disintegrated. Calgacus, mentioned by Tacitus as one of the leading figures in the last stand against Agricola at Mons Graupius, probably held a similar position and cannot be identified among the early names in the Pictish king lists.

The sovereignty of individual tribes or states is a highly emotive issue and works very effectively against their union to form larger national or supranational units. In mid-1990s Britain, one has only to listen to contemporary discussion about the European Community or European Monetary Union to realize that this is as true today as it has ever been. We hear very little about what might or might not be good for Europe as a whole, but a great deal about whether a particular move would be good for Britain or how it will affect the French farmers, and even more about potential dangers to British sovereignty and the possible undermining of the authority of the British Parliament.

Tribes, states and nations are like biological species: they have an inbuilt instinct for self-preservation. Species achieve this aim by efficient breeding, effective defence against predators and optimizing their use of the available food supply. Species that fail in this constant battle to remain in tune with an often changing environment go under. In the distant past the human species found that tribes could cope with the environment better than smaller family units. Tribes then became biologically desirable for the species. Problems arose, however, when the species became so successful that tribes began to clash with one another for possession of their share of the environment. This was not good for the species, but the instinct for tribal preservation was so firmly implanted that it could not be overcome. It was as if the members of each tribe had become one species, while the members of other tribes (foreigners) were viewed as another species, either (to continue the biological analogy) predators or prey. Warfare, whether defence against predatory tribes or attack on other tribes, has been with us ever since.

Sovereignty is the problem that has to be overcome if a nation is to be formed by the amalgamation of smaller tribal units. A common solution to this problem was to have two levels of kingship: a high king over the whole nation and lesser kings over each of the tribes. This ensured the preservation of the tribes as recognizable entities within the larger nation, and also provided for their representation at the national court. Thus, in eighth- and ninth-century England, the lesser kingdoms of Kent, Sussex, Essex and East Anglia generally acknowledged the overlordship of a greater king, such as Offa of Mercia or Alfred of Wessex, but there was no system for deciding who should be such a king of England. The Wessex dynasty was finally established in this position because they happened to have the strongest kings at the time of the Danish invasions. Had these invasions begun a century earlier, the kings of England might well have been Mercian rather than West Saxon.

In Wales the situation was considerably worse. While it was sometimes possible for an individual king to establish his authority over most of the country, it was almost impossible to derive any permanent benefit from such an achievement. Rhodri Mawr (844–78) began his reign as King of Gwynedd. His mother was a sister of the King of Powys, and he himself married a sister of the King of Ceredigion. When the King of Powys died in 855, Rhodri took over; and he repeated the performance when his brother-in-law, the King of Ceredigion, died in about 872. Thus when he died his kingdom covered a very large part of Wales. But he had six sons and his possessions were divided between them according to the custom of gavelkind which was prevalent in Wales at the time.[1] What possible chance was there for a united kingdom of Wales?

The Picts, unlike the English or the Britons, chose their kings from the female royal line. This practice, for which we have the contemporary authority of Bede, is fully consistent with the evidence of the Pictish king lists. The kings in the lists are almost all identified by their fathers' names: Brude son of Maelchon, Nechtan son of Derile, and so on. With the exception of two of the last Pictish kings before Kenneth mac Alpin, not one of these kings succeeded his father to the throne. Apart from the importance of the female royal line, Bede's statement also suggests that the Picts (or more probably the kings of the various Pictish tribes) had some control over the choice of their overlord, the King of the Picts. Was this the secret of their success? Was this how they managed to establish a stable Pictish nation in such a relatively short time? Or did 'the fact that a father was not succeeded by his son . . . militate against the development of a strong monarchy and . . . therefore impair the effectiveness of the central authority'?[2]

If matrilinear succession was indeed so detrimental to political stability, why did the Picts adopt the practice? One suggestion is that it was an ancient custom surviving from the aboriginal (non-Celtic) Bronze Age inhabitants of Scotland.[3] Such a suggestion, by its very nature, can be neither proved nor disproved. Another suggestion relates to the supposed sexual habits of the tribes of Caledonia, as reported for example by Dio Cassius: 'they dwell in tents, naked and unshod, possess their women in common, and in common rear all the offspring'.[4] In such circumstances 'matrilinearism may have been adopted simply as a solution to the practical problem of proving paternity'.[5] The fact that in the Pictish king lists and the Irish annals the Picts (whether or not they were kings) were almost invariably identified as the sons of their fathers surely gives the lie to this slur on the habits of their ancestors.

If, as has sometimes but not universally been suggested, succession through the female line is a distinctively non-Celtic practice, it does not necessarily follow 'that the Picts, or rather certain elements among the Picts, were non-Celtic or non-Indo-European'.[6] They may have made a conscious and unilateral decision to adopt matrilineal succession for their kings, quite regardless of the fact that their Celtic and other Indo-European neighbours might view such a practice as unnatural; and they may have done so for sound political reasons. They may have spotted a weakness in the 'normal' succession of kings from father to son and decided to experiment with an alternative method.

In order to examine this possibility, we need to cast our minds back to the time, some time before the end of the third century, when no one (Roman or British) had ever heard of the Picts; a time when there were no such people. Caledonia was inhabited by a number of tribes – *Caledonii, Vacomagi, Venicones, Boresti, Decantae* and others – probably more than enough to match the seven sons of Cruithne. We sometimes refer to the people of these tribes, collectively and retrospectively, as proto-Picts, the people who one day, as if by an Act of Parliament, were suddenly to become the Picts. Ideally the new Pictish nation should not threaten the sovereignty of the tribes, nor should it seem to favour any one tribe over the others. If the first King of the Picts was chosen from among the tribal kings and, if the succession was to be from father to son, this would give a very clear advantage to the tribe and family of that first king; an advantage to which the kings of the other tribes might quite reasonably object. An alternative, which would avoid this situation, would be to arrange for the succession to follow the female line. On this system, when a king of the Picts died he would be succeeded by one of the following: his brothers, sons of his mother; his first cousins, sons of his mother's sisters; his nephews, sons of his own sisters; or perhaps his first cousins once removed, sons of his female first cousins. This would provide a wide range of suitably qualified candidates from whom the next king could be chosen. The potential benefits of such a system are summarized below.

1   The system posed no threat to the sovereignty of the tribes which joined the scheme, nor did it give any long-term benefit to the family or tribe of the ruling king.

2   The age range of candidates for the kingship would be considerable, probably as much as 30 or 40 years. Thus there was never the slightest need to choose a boy who was too young for the responsibility or a man who was too old and infirm to lead the nation effectively.

3   The number of candidates ensured that the kingdom need never be saddled with a king who was physically disabled or mentally unsound.

4   Unlike a modern election to choose a president or prime minister, the candidates for the Pictish kingship would have been recognized as such from birth and would be well known long before the old king died.

In the face of such clear advantages for a system of matrilinear succession, it is difficult to view the Picts as a nation whose political unity was 'permanently strained by a curious system of succession'.[7]

Apart from brothers, it is generally impossible to determine the relationship between successive Pictish kings. Their position was acquired through their mothers, but they are almost invariably named as the sons of their fathers. Considering their importance, it is remarkable how little we know of Pictish female royalty. In the *Annals of Ulster* there is a single reference to a Pictish princess, under the year 778, where the death of Eithni daughter of Cinadon is recorded. Cinadon was the 'Ciniod son of Wredech' in the *Pictish Chronicle*, who reigned for 12 years and whose death in 775 is also recorded in the *Annals of Ulster*.

About a quarter of the kings listed in the *Pictish Chronicle* were succeeded by their brothers: a high proportion, which might suggest that the 'electors' preferred to choose their kings from the close family of brothers and nephews (descendants of the king's mother) rather than the wider family of cousins (descendants of his grandmother). We shall of course never know. A matter of greater importance is the choice of husbands for the Pictish princesses. What sort of men were considered to be desirable fathers for possible future Pictish kings? Very few of the fathers can be identified with any certainty, and opinion has varied on the relative importance of foreign and Pictish marriages.

One of the few known fathers was Eanfrid, a member of the Northumbrian royal family, whose career is noted in some detail by Bede.[8] He spent 17 years in exile among the Picts during the reign of his uncle Edwin (617–33). While he was with the Picts he was converted to Christianity and baptized. On the death of Edwin he returned home and became King of Bernicia, while his cousin Osric became King of Deira.

No sooner had they come to their respective thrones than these two abandoned their Christian faith and returned to the old pagan ways. Within a year both were dead and the whole of Northumbria overrun by Cadwallon King of Gwynedd. So hateful was the memory of that disastrous year that 'all those calculating the reigns of kings have agreed to expunge the memory of these apostate kings and to assign this year to the reign of their successor King Oswald, a man beloved of God'.[9] Talorgan son of Enfret (variously spelt, Anfrait, Enfreth, Anfrait, Ainfrit, etc), King of the Picts, reigned for 4 years and died, according to the Irish annals, in 657.

The only other father of a Pictish king who can be identified with any certainty is Beli son of Neithon, King of the Strathclyde Britons, whose capital was at Dumbarton (Alclyde). Brude son of Bile was the great Pictish king who defeated an invading Northumbrian army at the battle of Nechtansmere. The earliest reference to this relationship is given in an Irish life of St Adomnan, Abbot of Iona.[10] The body of Brude son of Bile, who died in 693 according to the Irish annals, was carried to Iona where Adomnan watched over it through the night. So great was the abbot's grief over the death of the king that he was tempted, so we are told, to perform a miraculous cure and bring him back to life. The next day, when a passing holy man saw the body beginning to move and open its eyes, he urged Adomnan not to raise the king from the dead, on the grounds that it would be very bad for the morale of other priests who might not be able to repeat the miracle. The story ends with eight lines of verse represented as the words of Adomnan, presumably part of a funeral oration, as there is a reference to the oak coffin: 'a hollow stick of withered oak is about the son of the king of Alcluaith'.

Maelchon, the father of the powerful Pictish king Brude who was baptized by St Columba in about 565,[11] has sometimes been identified with Maelgwn King of Gwynedd, who died in 547.[12] But though there is no chronological objection to this suggestion, there seems to be no historical evidence to support it. Furthermore, although the evil ways of Maelgwn were well publicized by Gildas,[13] it is unlikely that he and his family were not, at least nominally, Christians. If Brude was really his son, would he have required baptism from St Columba?

Apart from these three, the fathers of the Pictish kings could hardly be more obscure. Even the names are unfamiliar, quite apart from the individuals who bore them. If the names of the kings and their fathers are listed separately, it will be observed that the two lists have very few names in common. This curious fact, which was long ago noted by Skene,[14] might be taken as evidence that the fathers were generally foreigners and the sons were given Pictish names by their Pictish (female royal line) mothers. And yet, if this were the case, we would expect more of the fathers to be recognizable members of the dynasties of neighbouring nations (Scottish, Irish, British, English). If, on the other hand, the fathers were mainly Pictish, why do so few of the names in the list of fathers appear in the list of kings' names? Possibly the kings chose new names at the time of their coronation, names maybe of heroes of old like Drust son of Erp, who reigned for a hundred years and fought a hundred battles, or of well-known kings like Brude son of Maelchon, who was baptized by St Columba. Such an explanation might account for the preponderance of a small number of specially favoured names in the list of kings.

To return to the Pictish princesses and the question of their potential marriage partners, we must remember that, at any one time, there would have been several such ladies (sisters and daughters, and maybe granddaughters and cousins of the king) for whom husbands were to be found. Any unmarried kings and princes of the various Pictish tribes would surely have been high on the list of eligible young men. Such choices would ensure that the royal blood flowed through the veins of all the tribal kings, that all those kings had an equal place in the councils of the Pictish nation, and that each tribe had an equal chance of providing a king of the Picts. This would clearly work for the political stability of the nation. If a marriage was arranged with a foreign prince, this would not necessarily lead to a risk of the Picts coming under the rule of a foreign king. No one princess was any more likely to give birth to a king of the Picts than any other. The choice was made when the throne fell vacant, not when the mother of an unborn son was married.

Far from being a story without foundation invented or perpetuated by Bede, far from being a quaint custom inherited from Bronze Age ancestors, and far from being necessitated by lax moral behaviour, the system of succession of the Pictish kings through the female royal line may well have been a very astute political scheme devised by the first architects of the Pictish nation – a scheme whereby a kingdom was created from diverse tribes in an extraordinarily short time, and was maintained for over five hundred years.

Alfred Smyth, who strongly opposed what he referred to as the 'matrilinear myth',[15] reached a very similar conclusion. He explained the lack of father to son succession in the Pictish king lists by suggesting that these lists are in reality lists of high kings or overlords and that the Picts operated a system (not detailed) whereby this office rotated among the tribal kings. The advantages of such a rotation, as he rightly pointed out, are 'that large confederacies can be held together in "nations" such as the Picts, with all the stronger tribal aristocracies assured a share in overlordship'. Bede, far from being the perpetrator of a matrilinear myth, was surely providing us with contemporary evidence of how the Picts operated their system of rotating overlordship.

CHAPTER 7

What were the Picts?

The question posed by Wainwright in *The Problem of the Picts* was 'Who were the Picts?'. This question seemed to imply that there was something distinctively Pictish about the Picts, some racial characteristic or characteristics that set them apart from neighbouring peoples, something distinctive about their build or their colouring; the language they spoke, the clothes they wore; their religion and customs; their history and prehistory. But Wainwright was careful to point out that he meant no such thing. Indeed after some discussion he concluded that, at the time of writing (1954), 'philologists, archaeologists and historians, differing among themselves at many points, would probably all agree that the historical Picts were a heterogeneous people and that the antecedents of Pictland should not be sought in a single race or culture'.[1]

If, instead of Wainwright's question, we ask, 'What were the Picts?', the answer is very simple. They were a nation created by the union of a number of tribes. This union, formed initially as a military alliance against the common enemy, stood the test of time and long outlived the threat of Roman invasion. For the last seventeen centuries the peoples of this union have been known collectively as the Picts, a name first recorded by the Romans. The name itself is a familiar part of the problem: did *Picti* really mean 'the painted men', or was it simply the Latin form of a long-forgotten native name? Putting this question on one side for the moment, we might refer to the Picts as 'The United Tribes of Caledonia', or UTC for short, a name which tells us just what they really were. The 'proto-Picts', the name coined for the peoples who were to become Picts in the third and fourth centuries,[2] would then have been the various different tribes occupying Caledonia at the time of the Roman invasion. We know the names of some of these tribes, mainly from Ptolemy's geography. What we want to know is something about their racial connections and origins.

In historical times, invasions and immigrations have taken place from three main directions:

1 by land from the south (Romans and English);
2 by sea from the west (Irish);
3 by sea from the north (Vikings).

Apart from the Romans, who failed to establish any permanent settlement north of the Antonine Wall, the footprints of these incomers have been indelibly

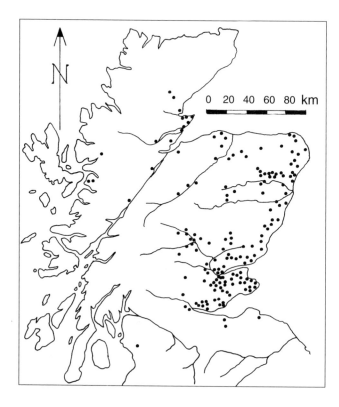

Distribution of Pit- place-names in mainland Scotland. The very few examples in the west (for which see Watson, 1926, p. 407) are no longer to be found on the 1 in 50,000 Ordnance Survey maps, and others may have disappeared without trace as a result of rural depopulation.

stamped on the map of Scotland in the form of place-names. By careful linguistic, geographical and historical analysis, a relative chronology of place-names can be built up, so that the layers can be stripped off like archeological strata in an excavation.[3]

Over much of eastern Scotland there is an important group of place-names which belongs to none of these historical incursions. Among these are some well-known names beginning with *Aber-*, such as Aberdeen, Abernethy and Arbroath (formerly Aberbrothoc). Aber, a British word meaning the mouth of a river or a confluence, where a tributary joins a major river, is also a common element in Welsh place-names, as in Aberystwyth, Aberdovey and Abergavenny, and is quite distinct from its Gaelic equivalent, *inver*. These names, and others like them, tell us something about the tribes of Caledonia before their union.

The most abundant and distinctive names of this group are those beginning with *Pit-*, such as Pitlochry and Pittenweem. *Pit*, originally *pett*, a Pictish word meaning a piece of land, is related to the Welsh word *peth*, meaning a thing, and the Breton *pez*, a piece.[4] The Gaelic equivalent *cuid*, meaning a portion, is quite distinct and does not appear as an element in place-names. Most of the *pit*-names still belong to individual farms rather than towns or villages, as befits their origin. There are some three hundred *pit*-names with a rather well-defined distribution, mainly north of the Forth, east of the Highlands and south of the Moray Firth. This area is the heartland of the Pictish kingdom, but certainly not the whole of

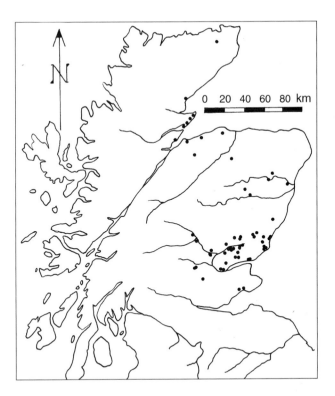

Distribution of Class II symbol stones in mainland Scotland, often compared with the distribution of Pit-place-names and, with them, used as an indicator of Pictish settlement.

it. Similarly, the words *aber* and *pett*, while certainly part of the Pictish language, were only a very small part of it. What these place-names really tell us is that a few words of the language spoken in a large part of the Pictish kingdom were related to the British language spoken in southern Britain.

The distribution of *pit*-names compares closely with that of the Pictish Class II symbol stones, those with relief carving. Chronologically and geographically, both are definitely Pictish, but to say that either of them is 'a valid indicator for the area of Pictish settlement in Scotland'[5] is simply not justified by the evidence. The perfectly reasonable statement that the Class II symbol stones were carved by the Picts does not imply that wherever there were Picts they were carving symbol stones in relief. The interpretation of these distributions – of *pit*-names and Class II symbol stones – may be aided by consideration of a third distribution pattern, the historical context of which is well known.

The Romans have no direct connection with *pit*-names or with Class II symbol stones, and yet the distribution of Roman forts and marching camps north of the Antonine Wall shows a remarkable similarity to that of pit-names and Class II symbol stones. Why? We know that the Romans invaded Scotland by land from the south, and that is the essential factor in the distribution of their forts. The *pit*-names and *aber*-names are related to the language of southern Britain. Maybe these represent a component of the Pictish language that reached Scotland by land from the south and was incorporated into the speech of some of the tribes of

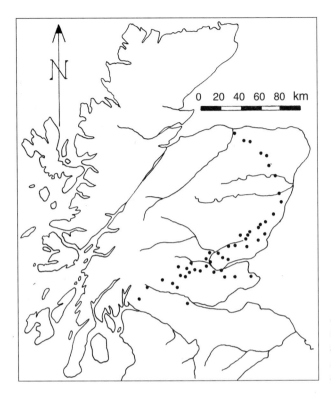

Distribution of Roman forts in mainland Scotland, showing similarity to the distribution of Pit- place-names and Class II symbol stones.

Caledonia. Perhaps the skill in relief carving on stone also came up by land from the south, as a result of Northumbrian influence, and was eagerly taken up by the Picts whose stone carving had previously been restricted to incised designs. The connection between Pictish and Northumbrian art has long been appreciated.

A further important fact about the *pit*-names is that the second component is almost invariably of Gaelic origin,[6] as in Pitcaple (from *capull* a horse or mare) and Pitcorthy (from *coirthe* a pillar or stone). If it is assumed that the Gaelic language did not reach eastern Scotland until the middle of the ninth century, 'when the king of the Scots, Kenneth MacAlpin, crushed Pictish resistance and united Pictland and Gaelic-speaking Scotland',[5] then we have to conclude that all these *pit*-names are post-Pictish hybrids. This would leave us with an extraordinary shortage of early place-names. The assumption is, however, quite unjustifiable. Whatever we may think of Kenneth mac Alpin and his dealings with the Picts, and however we interpret the names beginning with *Pit-* and *Aber-*, and a few others in the same category, the language of the Picts is still open to question, and no evidence has ever been presented that it did not contain a Gaelic component.

If we turn now to a consideration of Gaelic place-names, we immediately face a problem of selection. There are so many such names and they are so widespread that the difficulty lies in discovering a Gaelic root which might have some chronological significance. The Gaelic *sliabh*, meaning a mountain, was chosen by

Professor W.F.H. Nicolaisen because its restricted geographical distribution suggested that it had ceased to be used in the formation of place-names some time before Gaelic came to be spoken over most of the Scottish mainland.[7] In other words it is suggested that, although *sliabh* is still part of the Scottish Gaelic language, its occurrence in place-names is archaic. If this is true, the distribution of such place-names is of the greatest interest.

The greatest concentration of place-names beginning with *Sliabh-* is in the Rhinns of Galloway, where it is generally spelt *Slew-*, with a thin eastward spread towards Dumfries. Outside this limited area in south-west Scotland, *sliabh*-names occur in Kintyre and the adjacent islands (Islay, Jura and Arran), beyond which there is a further scatter in the Central Highlands, mainly in the upper reaches of the Spey and the Tay. This distribution is correlated with 'the known Dalriadic settlement and the first few centuries of expansion which followed it on the mainland'.[8] On this interpretation the concentration of *slew*-names in Galloway implies a similar Irish colonization of that area, which, though by no means unlikely in view of the short sea crossing, seems to have gone unrecorded in history or tradition.

There are several weak points in this interpretation. First, the four names in mainland Argyll can hardly be considered a very good Dalriadan concentration. Second, a spread from this initial colony across into Pictland, whether of people or their language, is hardly likely to have taken place across some of the highest

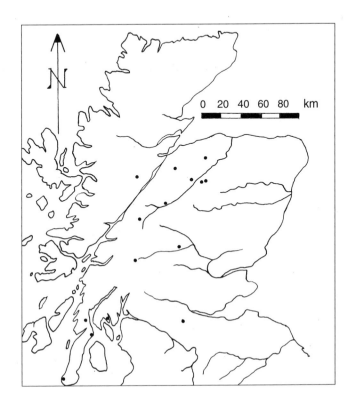

Distribution of Sliabh-place-names in mainland Scotland north of the Forth–Clyde line.

mountain areas in Scotland and down into the river valleys beyond. Third, once again using Roman forts and camps as indicators of the main lines of communication through Scotland, the distribution of *sliabh*-names north of the Antonine Wall and *slew*-names south of it begins to look much more like a residual pattern than a growth pattern. If this is so, these names, far from representing the spearhead of an eastward linguistic thrust from Ireland, may in fact be the exact opposite; they may be old fashioned names, only used in remote western areas, far from the centres of cultural, political and linguistic activity and change. The best area to test this hypothesis is in southern Scotland, where the distribution of Gaelic place-names is marginal to a concentration of datable early English names.

Early English place-names, such as Coldingham, Abington, Polwarth and Borthwick, can be dated on linguistic and historical evidence to the period of Northumbrian expansion, between about 650 and 850.[9] The greatest concentration of these names in Scotland is in the lower Tweed valley and its tributaries. North of this, early English names spread round the coast to North Berwick and along the passes through the hills towards Edinburgh. This looks like a growth pattern on the map and corresponds with the known expansion of Northumbrian influence into Scotland. There are a few Gaelic names, such as Ballencrieff and Balgone, in the North Berwick area, the *bal-* root being the Gaelic equivalent of the Pictish *pit-*, and there are also British names in the same area, for example Aberlady. Unlike the English or British names in this area, however, the Gaelic names are quite isolated. Similarly, the few *bal-* names in the Tweed valley area are way up in the hills, far from each other and far from the mainstream of contemporary life. This is just the situation where we would expect the earliest linguistic stratum of an area to be preserved. It is not possible to put a date on such names, but their distribution looks residual. It is as if the incoming Northumbrians and, before them, the incoming Britons had pushed an earlier Gaelic-speaking population (or at least their language) into the marginal hill-farming country. Further west, away from the early Northumbrian influence, Gaelic place-names are abundant, as they are in the north. Here the intrusive element is Scandinavian and is related to Viking colonization of the area around the Irish Sea.

In the south-western counties the most obvious Norse contribution to the map is the large number of hills called 'fells'. Alongside these are many English 'hills' and Gaelic 'knocks'. In contrast to this the rarity of Norse settlement names is somewhat surprising. In and around Dumfriesshire there is a local concentration of Norse place-names ending in *-by* or *-bie* (Lockerbie) and *-thwaite*, but elsewhere such names are extremely rare.[10] This can only mean that Norse influence in the south-west (outside the Dumfriesshire area) did not upset the local settlement pattern or the place-names associated with it. The conclusion that the Gaelic place-names beginning with *Bal-* and *Auch-* are earlier than the Viking invasion is supported by hill names such as Balmurrie Fell, where the hill has been named after a nearby settlement with a Gaelic name.[10]

Another area with a well-dated group of intrusive place-names is the far north-east, around Thurso, Wick and John o'Groats. Here, early Scandinavian place-

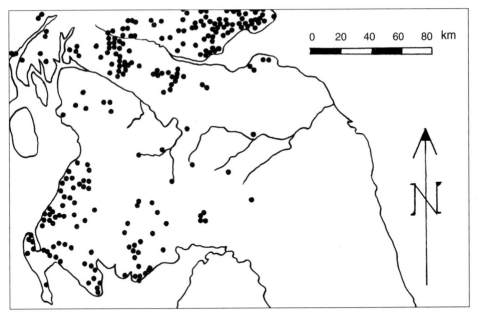

0   20   40   60   80 km

Distribution of Bal- place-names in southern Scotland.

names, such as Nybster, Scrabster, Seater and Reaster, can be dated to the last few decades of the ninth century,[10] when Caithness, together with Orkney, was lost to the Viking invaders. For the next four centuries, the whole of Caithness formed a mainland extension of the Norwegian earldom of Orkney. Perhaps the most remarkable thing about the distribution of early Scandinavian place-names in north-eastern Scotland is that it is limited to such a small area. To the west and to the south these Scandinavian names quickly give way to Gaelic names beginning with *Bal-* and *Ach-*, with some hybrid names such as Achlibster and Achscrabster in the contact zone. The conclusion seems inescapable that the Norse language became the common speech of the people only in the extreme north-east and, furthermore, that the language spoken in the rest of Caithness was Gaelic. Four hundred years of Norse rule had remarkably little impact on the language spoken by the people of Caithness. Can we seriously suppose that these same people gave up their native Pictish speech for the Gaelic language in the few short and tumultuous decades following the union of the Scottish and Pictish kingdoms under Kenneth mac Alpin, or should we conclude that they spoke Gaelic throughout the period of Pictish domination and went on speaking Gaelic under the Norwegians?

What the place-names seem to be telling us is that, wherever a chronology can be worked out, the Gaelic language was well established before the historical incursions of the Northumbrian Angles and the Vikings. In eastern Scotland in the heartland of the Pictish kingdom, and south of the Antonine Wall in the historical British kingdoms, Gaelic place-names are accompanied by names with British roots. It is difficult on the place-name evidence alone to work out a chronological sequence for the British and Gaelic languages. The existence of so many hybrid names implies that, for a considerable time, elements from both languages were in use together, and this is confirmed by Bede in his description of the eastern end of the Antonine Wall, which begins 'at a place which the Picts call Peanfahel and the English Penneltun'.[11] Peanfahel is a British–Gaelic hybrid meaning 'the end of the wall',[12] while the contemporary Penneltun is a British–(Gaelic)–English hybrid. By the twelfth century the British root in this name had been replaced by its Gaelic equivalent, and the place is now called Kinneil. The history of this one place-name is an interesting example of the resurgence of the Gaelic language after the formation of the 'modern' Scottish kingdom.

It is widely believed that the Gaelic language was first introduced into Scotland from Ireland in the fifth century by the Dalriadan settlers in Argyll, and that it completely ousted the (non-Gaelic) Pictish language some four hundred years later, after the union of the kingdoms under Kenneth mac Alpin. The greatest difficulty with this hypothesis is in south-west Scotland, in the Galloway area, which remained under British rule until the middle of the tenth century. There seems to be neither time nor reason for a late adoption of the Gaelic language there. Indeed it is much more likely that an early predominantly Gaelic language survived in this area through centuries of British rule, much as the British language survived in Brittany under French rule, and in Cornwall under English

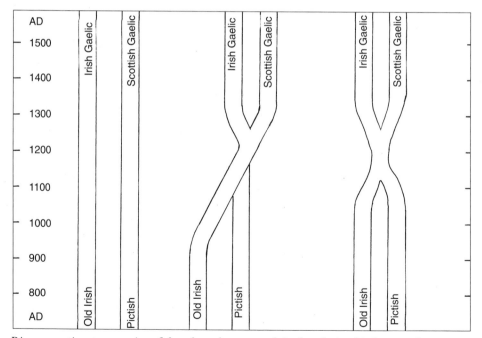

Diagrammatic representation of three hypotheses to explain the relationship between the (ancient) Pictish and (modern) Scottish Gaelic languages: according to Skene (left), Jackson (middle), and this book (right).

rule. If language had been more closely linked to political dominance, Chaucer, Shakespeare and Scott would never have written in English.

The belief that the Gaelic language did not arrive in Scotland until the Dalriadan settlement in the late fifth century is an assumption which, by frequent and authoritative repetition, has become established as a pseudo-fact. The contrary view, that an early form of the Gaelic language was spoken throughout Scotland many centuries earlier and developed into modern Scottish Gaelic, was popularized by Skene more than 150 years ago, but is now very much out of favour. As Professor K.H. Jackson said in an important paper on the Pictish language, 'not a single philologist of standing has supported Skene's opinion, and the voice of Celtic scholars has been unanimous in condemning it'.[13] Professor Nicolaisen, in his book on Scottish place-names, was just as adamant that 'disagreement has to be voiced with the idea that Gaelic must have been established in Galloway before the Cumbric [British] period'.[14]

The difficulty with a pre-Dalriadan Gaelic language in Scotland stems from two quite different sources. First, we know on the contemporary authority of Bede that the Pictish and Scottish (Dalriadan) languages were quite distinct, and Bede's statement receives further support from Adomnan's *Life of St Columba*, where it is recorded that Columba had to speak to the Picts through an interpreter.[15] Second, the modern Scottish and Irish Gaelic languages, still very close to one another, can be traced back to an ancestral 'Common Gaelic' which did not begin to split up until the thirteenth century.[16] If these two statements are

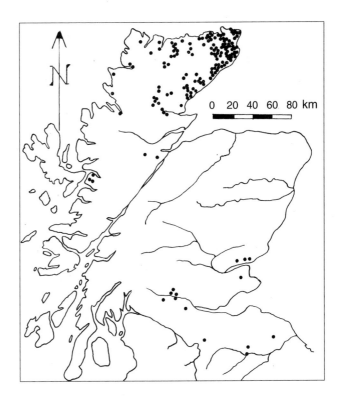

Distribution of brochs on mainland Scotland. Were these remarkable drystone castles built by aboriginal proto-Picts, free from 'foreign' influences?

Dun Telve broch, Gleann Beag, south-east of Glenelg. Above: external structure from the north-west; below: internal structure from the east.

accepted, the conclusion that the Pictish language ultimately gave way to this Common Gaelic language is inescapable. This, however, tells us nothing whatever about the nature of the Pictish language. As Jackson stressed in his paper on the evolution of the Goedelic (Gaelic group) languages, 'this does not necessarily mean that there cannot have been tribes speaking a Goedelic language living in Scotland (and for that matter in England too) in the last millenium before Christ and later . . . The point is that if there were, and this has never yet been proved, then their language died out without leaving any literary traces.'[17]

With these linguistic considerations in mind, we can now return to the evidence of the place-names. The simplest interpretation is that in late prehistoric times, towards the end of the first millenium BC, a Goedelic language (so called to distinguish it from the much later Common Gaelic and Irish and Scottish Gaelic languages) was spoken over the whole of Scotland. This Goedelic language was modified by the influence of the Brittonic language of southern Britain, an influence felt most strongly in southern Scotland and in eastern Scotland north of the Firth of Forth. This Brittonic influence came to an end with the Roman invasion of Scotland under Agricola and the subsequent building of Hadrian's Wall and the Antonine Wall. North of the Antonine Wall the resultant blend of Goedelic and Brittonic tongues evolved for several centuries, isolated from the nascent British language of the south by the Roman occupation and from the developing Irish language to the west by the great mountain barrier which extended southwards as far as the Firth of Clyde. This hybrid speech developed over the centuries into the distinctive Pictish language, a language neither truly British nor fully Gaelic.

Further south the forces of change were stronger, first British, then Roman and finally English. The most vulnerable area, mainly east of a line from Edinburgh to Carlisle, became linguistically, and for a time politically and culturally, a northward extension of Northumbrian England. Further west the British kingdoms of Strathclyde and Rheged maintained their independence for some time after the union of the Pictish and Scottish kingdoms. Judging from the place-names, however, the inhabitants of these western kingdoms probably continued to speak a hybrid Gaelic–British language, much like that of the Picts. The possible survival of this language may even have prompted twelfth-century references to the (contemporary) Picts of Galloway, who have given rise to so much discussion.[18] The ultimate fate of the Pictish language, as of the people who spoke it, will be considered in chapter 15.

As a clue to the ethnic origins of the tribes of Caledonia, which combined with such outstanding success to form the Pictish nation, the place-names and the language which gave rise to them must be considered a great disappointment. Whatever original differences there may have been between the tribes of Caledonia, by the time the earliest surviving place-names were being established they were all speaking much the same (Pictish) language. Indeed their similarities may always have exceeded their differences. Tacitus, presumably on the good authority of his father-in-law Agricola, wrote that the Caledonians were a race apart from the inhabitants of southern Britain. In contrasting their red hair and large limbs with the swarthy faces and curly hair of the *Silures* of far off South

White Caterthun hillfort, near Brechin. Above: interior showing tumbled stone rampart; below: outer rampart and ditch.

Wales,[19] Tacitus may be implying a racial purity for these two such as was not to be found among the intervening tribes.

In the archaeological record, the most prominent division in Caledonia in the latest prehistoric period is that between the fort builders and the broch builders. The forts have a generally eastern distribution, very similar to that of the British place-names. The brochs have a mainly northern and north-eastern distribution on the mainland, extending also down the western coastal strip. Offshore, they are most abundant in Orkney and Shetland and, to a lesser extent, in the Hebrides. The brochs were an entirely native development and their distribution, in the furthest extremities of the land, was largely beyond the reach of the cultural and linguistic influences of southern Britain. The geographical isolation of the broch builders does not, however, make them any more 'aboriginal' than their neighbours further south. Eventually, their descendants joined the United Tribes of Caledonia and became, for a time, Picts; though their language might not have been recognized as Pictish by Bede's Northumbrian contemporaries.

This chapter ends as it began. The Picts were a nation created by the union of a number of tribes; but as far as their racial origin or origins are concerned, we remain completely in the dark. Place-names and archaeology may tell us something about the cultural connections of the people who became Picts, but cultural connections are a far remove from ethnic identity.

CHAPTER 8

Who were the Scots?

Who were the Scots? What sort of a question is this? The problem of the Picts is well known and it would be perfectly in order to make yet another attempt to answer the age-old question: 'Who were the Picts?' But we all know who the Scots were. They came over from Ireland towards the end of the fifth century, under the leadership of Fergus mac Erc and his brothers, and founded the Scottish kingdom of Dalriada; or, perhaps more correctly, they extended their Irish kingdom of Dalriada (in County Antrim) to include that part of Scotland which later became known as Argyll. Not surprisingly, they spoke the Irish (Gaelic) rather than the British (Welsh) language. Indeed an early (1165) form of Argyll was Arregaithel or Arregaichel, meaning 'the district of the Gaels',[1] presumably so called in contrast to the Pictish country east of the mountains. So what is the problem?

The Scots first came to the notice of the outside world in the fourth century AD, when they allied themselves with the Picts in their devastating raids on Roman Britain. The continuation of those raids into the fifth century was recorded by the near contemporary British historian Gildas, whose work provided the source for much of Bede's knowledge of early British history. To the classical writers, and to Gildas, Bede and Nennius, all writing in Latin, these people were known as *Scotti*. Bede was the first to write of them as inhabitants of neighbouring parts of the British Isles and not simply as unwelcome raiders of the territory formerly occupied by the Romans. From Bede we learn that the Scots were the native race of Ireland and that the Scots of northern Britain had come over from Ireland under the leadership of a chieftain called Reuda, after whom they were still (i.e. in 731) called Dalreudians.[2] Because of the possibility of confusion, Bede was careful, wherever necessary, to distinguish between the Scots who lived in Britain and the Scots of Ireland.[3]

Bede's Scottish chieftain, Reuda, appears in the genealogy of William the Lion, King of Scotland (1165–1214) as Echdach Riada, thirteen generations earlier than Fergus mac Erc.[4] Like Cruithne, the ancestor of the Picts, Echdach Riada's family was by this time traced back through many generations to Jafeth, son of Noah. Echdach (Echoid) Riada was supposed, according to Irish tradition, to have led his people out of south-western Ireland at a time of famine, and settled them in northern Britain and north-eastern Ireland.[5] Another interesting character in the genealogy of William the Lion is Goildil-glais (Gaidelus) son of Neuil (Neolus), represented as being the twenty-second generation from Jafeth son of Noah.

Gaidelus was said to be a nobleman of Scythia, from which the names Scita, Scitius, Scoticus, Scotus and Scotia were derived;[6] and Gaidelus himself gave his name to the language spoken by the Scots. As if all this were not enough, Gaidelus was said to have married Scotta, generally referred to as daughter of Pharaoh, King of Egypt, thus providing a more convincing etymology for the Scots.[7] Gaidelus and his people travelled in many countries and eventually settled in Spain, whence their descendants migrated to Ireland. According to Nennius, who had consulted the best scholars among the Scots (Irish), they arrived in Dal Riada '1002 years after the Egyptians had been drowned in the Red Sea'.[8] With minor variations (and generally without the precise dating given by Nennius), this was the story which would have been told in the Middle Ages, if anyone had wanted to know who the Scots were.

Of course all this is not history, at least not in the modern sense, but it is nonetheless of considerable interest. It tells us how the early historians coped with the problem of how to begin their story. Nowadays we rely on the evidence of archeology and use the prehistoric periods as a general introduction to history. When we come to the Dark Ages, the rather diffuse boundary zone between prehistory and history, archeology is supplemented by other methods, including the study of place-names, as seen in the last chapter. A similar motivation must have prompted early attempts to relate the names of peoples and countries to their more distant past. The first tentative suggestions in this direction could easily have been incorporated in the oral tradition and, when this was later committed to writing, would have taken on the aura of established fact.

These early stories were easily accepted because they fitted a model of history which was based on observation. All over the known world, people were on the move. In Britain the Romans had come and gone and the English had come to stay, and elsewhere in Europe there were the Franks, the Goths, the Visigoths and others, all swarming over the tattered remains of the Roman Empire. In such an age it was reasonable to suppose that the various peoples of Britain had originated by migration, with or without military invasion, from some older country. A similar model of prehistory was extremely popular among archeologists until quite recently.[9] The essential truth of this model became very clear when conversion to Christianity brought with it the certain knowledge that the only people to be saved from the universal flood were Noah and his immediate family. The whole world must therefore have been populated by the migration of his descendants.

With this medieval view of history in mind, we can return to Fergus mac Erc and his brothers, and look at the evidence for their colonization of Argyll. One of the earliest surviving accounts is in the *Duan Albanach*[10], a poem listing the reigns and achievements of the Scottish kings, composed during the reign of Malcolm Canmore (1057–93). The poet began with a rhetorical question which immediately tells us that he is using the migration and invasion model of history.

> O all ye learned of Alban
> Ye well skilled host of yellow hair
> What was the first invasion – is it known to you?
> Which took the land of Alban?

Alban, originally the name of the whole of Britain, was restricted to northern Britain after the Roman occupation had effectively split the country in two. Having posed the question, the poet went on to provide us with the answer: Albanus, son of Isacon and brother of Briutus, was the first to possess it, and named it after himself. This story is based on a British foundation story which probably originated during the Roman occupation, when Virgil's *Aeneid* would have had an important place in the schooling of aspiring young citizens of Roman Britain. In Virgil's epic, Aeneas has two sons, Ascanius, the founder of Alba Longa, and Silvius, the ancestor of the later Alban kings. Maybe some British student, on reading the introductory sentence, 'this was the beginning of the Latin race, the Alban fathers and the high walls of Rome',[11] thought that the 'Alban' referred to his own country. Or maybe it was just the appearance of the name Brutus in book 6.[12] Whatever the reason, the British foundation story, taken, as Nennius says,[13] from 'the Annals of the Romans', provides Silvius with a son called Brutus (or Britto), who is driven into exile and, after much journeying, reaches this island which he names Britain after himself. The author of the *Duan Albanach*, taking account of the division of Britain into north and south, provides Brutus with a brother, Albanus. The family of Brutus was further modified by Geoffrey of Monmouth, a few decades later, to account for the division of southern Britain into England and Wales.[14] In the *Duan Albanach*, Brutus and Albanus are said to be the sons of Isacon, which may be a corruption of Ascanius and therefore a slight deviation from the British story, in which Brutus is the son of Silvius.

The story of Brutus and Albanus does not end, as we might expect, with the naming of Alban, which was after all its main purpose. In the third verse the poet takes it a stage further:

> Briutus banished his active brother
> Across the stormy sea of Icht,
> Briutus possessed the noble Alban
> As far as the conspicuous promontory of Fotudain.

This seems not only very unfair to Albanus, but quite unnecessary. Albanus was brought into the story for the sole purpose of providing an explanation for the name of his country. Why banish him? And where was the conspicuous promontory of Fotudain? Did the poet think that this was one of the northern headlands, from Cape Wrath in the north-west to Duncansby Head, near John o' Groats, in the north-east? And was the stormy sea of Icht the Pentland Firth? Maybe the promontory of Fotudain was not a promontory at all but, in some earlier tradition, the tribe known as the *Votadini*, who lived in the country south of the Firth of Forth. It would have been perfectly reasonable to say that Brutus ruled Britain as far north as the *Votadini* and that Albanus ruled the country further north. Such a description would fit the historical boundary between the Britons and the Picts. Who can tell how many changes were made during the oral transmission of the poem which was eventually set down in writing as the *Duan Albanach* in the late eleventh century; how many changes were made and how many 'errors' introduced?

Long after Brutus, the poet continued, the race of Neimidh took Alban, under the leadership of Erglan. Then the Cruithnigh (Picts) took it afterwards, 'after coming from the plain of Erin'. The kings of the Picts are not listed in the *Duan Albanach*, but we are told that there were seventy of them from Cathluan to Cusantin. Cathluan is supposed to have been a contemporary of Cinge the father of Cruithne, but it is uncertain whether Custantin (Constantine) was the son of Fergus, who died in 820, or the son of Kenneth mac Alpin, who died in 872. Either way, the poet was clearly aware that there had been a long line of Pictish kings, the dates of whose reigns he did not know, and that this Pictish dynasty had somehow come to an end. He was faced with a problem that is still with us today. In the absence of contemporary records, how could he explain the end of the Pictish dynasty? The situation in his time was that there was a well-established dynasty of the kings of Alban, known in Latin and English as the kings of the Scots. Using his migration and invasion model of history, he could only conclude that the Scots must have taken Alban by force. The only question was who achieved this conquest and when. His answer is supplied in the sixth and seventh verses.

> The children of Eochad after them
> Took Alban, after great wars,
> The children of Conaire, the mild man,
> The chosen of the strong Gael.

> The three sons of Erc son of Eochaidh the valiant
> Three who obtained the blessing of Patrick,
> Took Alban, exalted their courage,
> Loarn, Fergus and Aongus.

The sixth verse is a genealogical statement that Fergus and his brothers were descendants of Eochad (Echdach Riada), son of Conaire, the founder of Dalriada. The seventh verse makes Fergus mac Erc and his brothers the conquerors of the whole of Alban, giving them the role of ending the Pictish dynasty and founding that of the Scots. This has nothing whatever to do with the colonization of Argyll from Ireland. It is quite clear that the poet is telling us about the succession of dynasties which he believed to have ruled over the whole of Alban.

A different solution to the same problem is provided in the tenth–century *Tripartite Life of St Patrick*.[15] Here Patrick is welcomed into the Irish territory of Dalriada by the twelve sons of Erc. In this story of the meeting, Patrick is made to prophesy a great future for Fergus and his descendants: 'From thee the kings of this territory shall for ever descend, and in Fortrenn. And this was fulfilled in Aedan, son of Gabran, who took Alban by force.' Aedan, son of Gabran, was great grandson of Fergus mac Erc and a contemporary of St Columba. Once again it seems clear that a conquest of the whole of Alban is implied, followed by the foundation of a Scottish dynasty. It is quite clear from the silence of the contemporary Irish annals that such a conquest never took place. It is simply another story invented to explain the replacement of the Pictish dynasty by the kings of the Scots.

As Marjorie Anderson said in her book, *Kings and Kingship in Early Scotland*, 'the traditions about the earliest DalRiatan settlement of Britain do not inspire great confidence'.[16] If anything this is an understatement. The traditions do not relate to an early Dalriadan settlement of Argyll at all, but to a hypothetical conquest of the whole of Alban. The conquering heroes were chosen from among the kings of Dalriada because they were already well known for other reasons: Fergus through his connection with St Patrick and Aedan through a much closer and better documented connection with St Columba.[17] Fergus, rather than being the leader of a Dalriadan invasion of Argyll, may have been remembered originally as the first Christian king of Dalriada.[18] The migration and invasion model for the Dark Age history of Scotland has been in vogue for more than a thousand years. Perhaps it is time at least to consider some other hypothesis.

It is quite clear from the distribution of prehistoric sites that the area which was to become the Scottish kingdom of Dalriada, and later still the county of Argyll, was well populated from the earliest times. It is the only such area along the whole of the western seaboard, from Cape Wrath right the way down to the Clyde. The reason for this lies in the geology and physical geography of the area. The underlying rocks are mainly soft slates and phyllites and, as a result, the hills are much gentler and the coastline less precipitous than elsewhere in the west. Is it possible that, without any invasion or colonization, the people of this part of the south-west Highlands developed a culture and language more akin to that of the Scots across the sea than that of the Picts across the mountains?

Adomnan, in his *Life of St Columba*, written towards the end of the seventh century, referred to 'the mountains of the spine of Britain' as forming the boundary between the Picts and the Scots in Britain.[19] The extent of this uninhabited mountain barrier is very clearly seen on the map of prehistoric sites. Even today very few roads cross this spine of Britain, and in the sixth and seventh centuries the best route was along the Great Glen, between Fort William and Inverness, travelling by boat along Loch Lochy and Loch Ness. Adomnan refers to St Columba's 'first tiring expedition' to visit Brude, the King of the Picts.[20] Crossing the spine of Britain was quite clearly not a journey to be undertaken lightly. Cultural exchange across such a barrier must have been minimal. The Picts to the east of the mountains were exposed to various influences from the south: British, Roman, and English in historical times, and perhaps others in earlier periods. The diffusion of such influences, apart from the movement of the incoming people themselves, could take place easily across well-populated country but would come to a halt when an unpopulated area was reached. The uninhabited mountainous spine of Britain was thus a very real barrier to the dissemination of cultural change.

The sea crossing between Ireland and Scotland seems to have presented no such barrier to communication. Journeys might be delayed by unfavourable winds, or rendered dangerous by storms, but sooner or later patience, perhaps with the help of a timely miracle, would be rewarded by a favourable wind and the ship would cross 'with full sails through all the seas' or 'thus with no labour' the journey would be rapid and prosperous.[21] Journeys by sea, whether between Ireland and Scotland or from island to island off the coast, were commonplace.

Adomnan made frequent reference to sailors and ships, and the winds from different quarters, each with its special name. It is abundantly clear that, by comparison with the spine of Britain, the sea was no barrier at all.

Whatever the ultimate origin of the Scots of northern Britain, the physical nature of their surroundings will have encouraged a cultural convergence between them and the Scots of Ireland, and a corresponding cultural divergence between them and the Picts. There is no need for an invasion from Ireland to explain their Gaelic speech or their general 'Irishness'. Indeed we might be persuaded to abandon the invasion hypothesis altogether, were it not for one remaining piece of documentary evidence, and that the earliest of all. In the second century AD, Ptolomey of Alexandria recorded a tribe called the *Epidii* in the area historically occupied by the Scots. From the name of the tribe it has been deduced that 'they must have spoken a P-Celtic language',[22] that is to say a British rather than a Gaelic type of Celtic. If this is true, then they are more likely to have been proto-Picts than proto-Scots, and an invasion from Ireland may be necessary to explain their replacement by the Dalriadan Scots. But is it true? Who told Ptolomey that they were called *Epidii*?

The original source of Ptolomey's information on the geography of Scotland was someone who had been there and recorded his observations, perhaps the commander of Agricola's fleet which circumnavigated Britain.[23] It is unlikely that such a voyage would have been undertaken without local guides who, apart from their knowledge of the coastal waters, would have been able to act as interpreters. In the first century such guides would most likely have come from southern Britain and would have given the names of places and tribes as they knew them. In other words the name *Epidii* might just as likely be an indicator of a P-Celtic interpreter as a P-Celtic tribe, and the 'real name' of the tribe might have been *Ecidii*. The possibility that the P-Celtic name *Epidii* existed alongside a contemporary Q-Celtic equivalent need cause no surprise. In South Wales there is a well-known early Christian tombstone inscribed in Latin: *Memoria voteporigis protictoris*. This is the memorial of Voteporix the Protector,[24] who is generally identified with the early sixth-century king known to Gildas as Vortiporius. His name might reasonably suggest that he and his people spoke a P-Celtic language, but there is also an Ogam inscription on the stone which contains the one word *Votecorigas*: (the stone) of Votecorix. The P-Celtic and Q-Celtic equivalents of this man's name existed quite literally side by side on his tombstone. In the light of this stone, Ptolomey's *Epidii* might equally well have been called *Ecidii*, and their name reveals absolutely nothing about either their language or their ethnic origin.

If Ptolomey's *Epidii* really referred to themselves as *Ecidii*, and this is pure speculation, we may perhaps indulge in a little medieval-style name matching, taking care to retain our twentieth-century critical faculties and realize that it can prove nothing. We have seen how often the names of founding ancestors were devised to fit with the names of tribes or countries: Brutus and Britain, Fib and Fife, Cait and Caithness, and so on. The founder of the kingdom of Dalriada, however, was not just called Riada (Bede's Reuda) but Eochaid Riada. The name Eochaid can be variously spelt – Echdach, Echoid, Echuid – and could very easily have been provided as an explanation of the tribal name *Ecidii*.

In a recent publication, *Invaders of Scotland*, the Scots take their well-established place alongside the Romans, the Angles and the Vikings, though the invasion itself is rather played down.[25] Some of these invasions are said to have been aggressive and others peaceful. As far as the Scots are concerned, 'current opinion favours a gradual settlement of *Scotti* from northern Ireland' during the fourth and fifth centuries. The invasion hypothesis dies hard. What is a peaceful invasion? How did a well-populated area such as Argyll manage to absorb a continuous flow of settlers from across the sea, over a period of two hundred years, without total disruption? Why did the Scots even consider settling in Argyll in a period when they and the Picts were allied in much more lucrative raids on the rich lands of Romanized southern Britain? It makes little sense and would not even bear consideration were it not for the fact that we have been indoctrinated with this invasion story for over a thousand years. Let us, like the prehistoric archeologists, dispense with the invasion hypothesis and see how the Scots of Argyll might have originated.

Without any invasion or settlement from Ireland, the proto-Scots, as we must call the ancestors of the Scots of Argyll, become one of the tribes of Caledonia. During the crucial centuries of their emergence into the light of history, their geographical isolation, west of the spine of Britain, was of fundamental importance. Unlike the tribes to the east of the mountains, they were not seriously threatened by the Roman invasions. They had no need to unite with the other tribes and sacrifice their sovereignty and their patrilinear succession of kings. Unlike these other tribes, they did not therefore 'become Picts', though it is perfectly possible that they were ethnically more 'Pictish' than 'Irish'. Thus separated from the proto-Picts by circumstances of geography and history, the proto-Scots established their cultural contacts across the Irish Sea. The reality of such contact is attested in the archeological record by imported artefacts. Without recourse to any invasions or migrations from Ireland, it is easy to see how the differences between the Picts and the Scots could have evolved by about AD 500.

CHAPTER 9

Out of the Mist: the Fifth Century

Among all the Pictish kings before Kenneth mac Alpin, only three (Drust son of Erp, Nechtan son of Erip and Brude son of Maelchon) had any of their deeds recorded in the group A version of the *Pictish Chronicle*.[1] The rest are mere time markers in the national chronology, their names accompanied by nothing more than the lengths of their reigns. Outside the pages of the *Pictish Chronicle* the first two are completely unknown to history. The third, Brude son of Maelchon, was well known beyond the confines of his own kingdom and was referred to by Bede and Adomnan, as well as the Irish annalists. What was so important about these three that they were selected for special treatment in the otherwise bare chronology of the Pictish kings?

We are told just three things about Drust son of Erp: he reigned for a hundred years and fought a hundred battles, and in the nineteenth year of his reign St Patrick arrived in Ireland. All of these 'facts' were set down in writing long after his death. His nicely rounded hundred year reign and exactly equivalent number of battles are the achievements of a folk hero, extracts from a story told and retold, and grown so much that the original is barely recognizable.

St Patrick's arrival in Ireland seems, at first sight, an unlikely event to be noted in the reign of a Pictish king. In Ireland, on the other hand, it was of such widespread significance that it provided an absolute baseline to which all other chronologies could be pegged. Thus in the early eleventh-century *Synchronisms of Flann Mainistreach* we read, 'Forty three years from the coming of St Patrick to Erin to the battle of Ocha. Twenty years from the battle of Ocha till the children of Erc, son of Echach Muindremhar, passed over into Alban.'[2] In this way the succession of Christian kings in various parts of Ireland, including the Dalriadan kings in Scotland, could be correlated with one another.

The first Christian missionaries from Ireland to the Picts must have had a strong sense of carrying on the work of St Patrick, and would have been well aware of the number of years that had elapsed since his arrival in Ireland. In view of the potentially comparable significance of their own journey, they would have done two things: back-calculated the date of St Patrick's arrival in Ireland, so that this important year could be fixed in the local chronology, and made sure that their own arrival was properly placed in the same scheme. If we accept the dating presented in Chapter 4, then Drust must have died in or around 478.[3] If we also accept 434 as the date for St Patrick's arrival in Ireland, as stated at the end of the 1187 version of the *Pictish Chronicle*,[4] then Drust must have come to the throne in about 416 and reigned for 62 years. While considerably short of the legendary hundred years, this would still have been an extraordinarily long reign, little short of Queen Victoria's record. The longest reign recorded for any subsequent Pictish king was 40 years for Constantine son of Aed (and grandson of Kenneth mac Alpin). Of course it is perfectly possible that the memory of Drust's long reign had already been exaggerated by the time the first missionaries arrived, in which case St Patrick's arrival in Ireland should be attributed to a correspondingly earlier year in his reign.

Drust was followed by Talore son of Aniel, whose reign lasted only 4 years, and then Nechtan son of Erip, who reigned for 24 years. In the third year of Nechtan's reign, Darlugdach Abbess of Kildare left Ireland on a mission to Britain. In the second year of her mission, Nechtan made her a grant of land at Abernethy, for God and St Brigid, whereupon she sang 'Alleluia'.[5] This is a record of the coming of Christianity to the Picts in about 486, little more than 50 years after the beginning of St Patrick's mission to Ireland and more than 70 years before the baptism of Brude son of Maelchon by St Columba. The group B version of the *Pictish Chronicle* makes no mention of Darlugdach's mission, and it is a reasonable deduction that the source of the group A version was a king list maintained in the church at Abernethy, whereas the group B version had its origin elsewhere.

The importance of St Darlugdach's mission to the Picts, and in particular to Abernethy, has been seriously underestimated or, more generally, totally ignored. There are three reasons for this:

1   the unfortunate tendency to regard records in the *Pictish Chronicle* before the reign of Brude 'as pre-historical in the sense that we know nothing about them from other sources';[6]
2   records of the building of the church at Abernethy about a hundred years later in the group B versions of the *Pictish Chronicle*;[7]
3   Bede's reference to the conversion of the southern Picts by St Ninian and the northern Picts by St Columba, which seems to imply that no other missions were involved.[8]

The group B versions of the *Pictish Chronicle*, the general unreliability of which has already been discussed in chapter 4,[9] do not give a consistent story about the building of the church at Abernethy. The relevant details are summarized below in a standardized format for ease of comparison.

Group B 1251 version:[10]
Gernerd son of Dompneth reigned for 20 years. Netthad son of Irb reigned for 21 years and built Abernethy. Kinet son of Luthren reigned for 14 years.

Group B 1187 version:[11]

Carnac son of Dormath reigned for 20 years and built Abernethy. Kynel son of Luthren reigned for 24 years.

Group B 1280 version:[12]
Garnald son of Dompnach reigned for 30 years and built the church of Abernethy 225 years and 11 months before the church of Dunkeld was built by Constantine king of the Picts. Kenech son of Sugthen reigned for 24 years.

Group B 1317 version:[13]
Gauiach son of Donath reigned for 20 years. Nactan son of Yrb reigned for 21 years. Kynel son of Luchrem reigned for 19 years.

The 1251 version attributes the building of Abernethy to Netthad (Nechtan) son of Irb, whereas the 1187 and 1280 versions omit this king altogether (perhaps a simple scribal error) and (probably as a result of this omission) give his predecessor the honour of building Abernethy. The 1317 version makes no mention of Abernethy or Dunkeld, though it does note the building of the church at St Andrews by Constantine son of Fergus, a building elsewhere attributed to his brother and successor, Oengus, and generally referred to by its earlier name of Kilremonth. The 1280 record of the building at Abernethy is clearly a late addition, foretelling as it does the building of Dunkeld 225 years and 11 months later! None of these building records displays any evidence of being either contemporary or reliable. The 1251 version does seem to preserve a tradition that Abernethy was built by a king called Nechtan son of Erip or something like that, but there is not the slightest reason for supposing that any of these group B stories should be accepted in preference to the group A record of Darlugdach's mission from Ireland.

Nechtan son of Erip, whose gift to Darlugdach is recorded in the group A versions of the *Pictish Chronicle*, is called in full 'Necton morbet filius Erip' in the 971–95 version, and the word *morbet* is given as *morbrec* or *mor breac* in the other versions. *Morbet* is meaningless, but *mor* (meaning great) and *breac* (meaning freckled) are Gaelic words. So 'Necton morbrec' was Nechtan the Great and was also nicknamed 'the freckled'. A Welsh king similarly nicknamed was Merfyn Frych, King of Gwynedd, who died in 844. In the group B versions of the *Pictish Chronicle*, Nechtan is given a completely different descriptive name, variously rendered as Nethan chelemot, Netthan thelchamoth, Nectane celtaniech and Nectan celchamoch. The first part of this word may well be the Gaelic *ceall* meaning a church, familiar in place-names such as Kilbride and Kilmarnock, the early form of the word being *cell*. Is it possible that the final syllable is the Gaelic *moch* (meaning early), and that the group B versions of the *Pictish Chronicle*, while failing to record Nechtan's initiative in welcoming Darlugdach's Christian mission, have nonetheless preserved a memory of that act in his descriptive name?

How does this record of Darlugdach's mission compare with Bede's statement that the southern Picts were said to have been converted by St Ninian? The centre of St Ninian's operations was at Whithorn in Galloway, which was famous in Bede's own time for its stonebuilt church dedicated to St Martin. St Ninian himself and many other saints were buried there.[14] Documentary evidence of St Ninian's activities further north is hard to find. The twelfth-century life of St Ninian himself, by Ailred of Rievaulx[15] gives no historical details beyond those already set down by Bede. A brief mention of St Ninian's mission north of Whithorn, however, is given in the life of St Kentigern by Jocelyn, Bishop of Glasgow, who died in 1199. When St Kentigern arrived in Glasgow, on his appointment as the first bishop of the Strathclyde Britons, he found there a Christian cemetery believed to have been consecrated by St Ninian.[16] Later in the book we read that the Picts had been converted in large part by St Ninian, but later lapsed into apostasy until they were converted again by St Kentigern.[17] The author then, carried away by enthusiasm for the achievements of his predecessor, goes on to say with unconvincing exaggeration that he converted not only the Picts, but also the Scots, and numerous other peoples in the far corners of Britain. If we accept this evidence of St Ninian's activity in Glasgow, the question remains: did his mission extend further north into southern Pictland?

Perhaps this question about St Ninian and the Picts might be rephrased: were the inhabitants of Galloway, between Whithorn and Glasgow, considered to be Picts in St Ninian's time? Several twelfth-century writers make historical references to the Picts of Galloway,[18] so that Jocelyn would very probably have considered St Ninian's work in Galloway as an early mission to the Picts. But the story of St Ninian and the Picts goes back to Bede in the early eighth century, and at that time the people of Galloway were thought of as Britons rather than Picts. Could the same people be Britons in one century and Picts in another and, if so, what were they in the fifth century, when St Ninian first converted them to Christianity? There are two distinct possibilities to be considered here:

1   the Pictish 'nation' at that time might actually have extended right across Galloway, as far as the Solway Firth;
2   the people of Galloway, while not being 'real' Picts in a political sense, might have been thought of as Picts by the inhabitants of southern Britain.

There is no indication anywhere in the *Pictish Chronicle* of the geographical extent of the Pictish kingdom. Our documentary sources for this are Bede (for the early eighth century) and the Pictish foundation stories of the seven sons of Cruithne and their territories (of uncertain chronological significance). There is no good reason why the boundaries of Pictland should have remained fixed for five centuries; indeed such stability would seem to be inherently unlikely. Neither source mentions Orkney or Shetland, and yet no discussion of the Picts would be considered complete without a mention of the St Ninian's Isle treasure of Shetland or the symbol stones of Orkney. For Orkney's place in the history of the Picts we have the testimony of Adomnan, that St Columba met a king of the Orcades who owed some sort of allegiance to Brude son of Maelchon, King of the Picts.[19] Some indication of the relationship between the two kings is given by the observation that Brude was holding hostages of the King of the Orcades. If Orkney and Shetland can be considered Pictish with such scant documentary evidence, why not Galloway also? And Pictish symbols are known from Galloway too, though not symbol stones in the usual sense.[20]

In the fifth century the rich farmers, villa dwellers and citizens of southern Britain lived under the constant threat of raids from the Picts and Scots. In earlier centuries their lifestyle had been supported by a strong central government and their property protected by the presence of the Roman army. Now the central government was crumbling and the Roman legions had crossed the channel for the last time, leaving Britain defenceless. Appeals to Rome had failed and the fateful decision was taken to employ Saxon mercenaries. But how much did the southern Britons know about the Picts? If asked where the Picts came from, what would they have answered – the pagan north; the barbarian north; north of Hadrian's Wall; somewhere north of York; the Caledonian Forest; north of the Solway Firth; or just up north? Any one of these answers would have been perfectly correct, and very few people in southern Britain would have been able to provide a more geographically specific answer. An educated Briton with an urge to travel would have been much more likely to cross the channel and visit Gaul than cross the wall and visit the land of the Picts. So when St Ninian set up his mission headquarters at Whithorn and began to convert the people in the surrounding country and further north, his work might well have been remembered in his own country as a mission to the Picts. Whether the people of Galloway were ever really Picts or whether they were no more than Picts by repute hardly seems to matter.

There is no evidence that St Ninian converted any of the Picts to the north of the Forth–Clyde line, and Bede's statement about his conversion of the southern Picts (presumably derived from a British source) is perfectly compatible with a mission restricted to the country between the Firth of Clyde and the Solway Firth. There seems not the slightest reason why we should not take the Picts' own record of Darlugdach's foundation at Abernethy at face value. As Smyth has said, 'this is a tradition which it was in nobody's interest ever to invent'.[22] Unfortunately he then proceeds to ignore the Pictish chronology and suggests that 'a date sometime about 625 for the founding of the Kildare colony at Abernethy would suit the Irish evidence very well'. Such a date is well over a hundred years too late for the Pictish evidence.

In the 971–95 version of the *Pictish Chronicle* the story of Nechtan, Darlugdach and Abernethy is considerably amplified in a paragraph[22] not found anywhere else. This paragraph must therefore be considered as an addition to this particular copy of the chronicle at some time which cannot easily be determined. It begins by giving Nechtan his full title, 'Nechtan the Great, son of Wirp, king of all the provinces of the Picts', and then goes on to relate that he granted Abernethy to St Brigid, 'in perpetuity to the day of judgement, with its territory, which is marked by a stone in Apurfeirt [Aberargie] through to a stone close to Ceirfuill [Carpow], that is, Lethfoss, and from there on to noble Athan [Hatton]'. The territory thus marked out represents some five square kilometres of prime farmland in the fertile floodplain of the River Earn, near its confluence with the Tay: a noble gift indeed. Little wonder that Darlugdach sang 'Alleluia' in response to King Nechtan's generosity. This document, which was never a part of the *Pictish Chronicle* proper and seems unlikely to be a medieval forgery, is most easily

View across the floodplain of the River Earn, north of Abernethy, showing some of the land granted by Nechtan son of Erip to Darlugdach for the foundation of the first Christian community in his kingdom.

interpreted as a record, kept in the church at Abernethy, of the property acquired at its foundation. If only those boundary stones were still standing, we might be able to examine some Pictish symbols in a documented historical context.

The circumstances which led to Darlugdach's foundation at Abernethy are of some interest and are briefly summarized after the description of the land granted to the church. Nechtan had been banished to Ireland by his brother Drust, and while over there had met St Brigid, the first Abbess of Kildare. He must have been impressed with her Christian religion and may even have been baptized by her. In any case, he asked her to plead with God on his behalf, and she told him that, if he managed to return to his own country, God would have mercy on him and he would hold the kingdom of the Picts in peace. That is all we are told. Should we treat the story as medieval fiction because there is no independent documentary evidence to back it up, or should we give it more serious consideration in relation to its historical context? Perhaps the first thing to note is that we are in reality dealing with two quite distinct documents, though both of them were presumably kept at Abernethy. The *Pictish Chronicle* gives a strictly chronological account of the momentous transactions between Nechtan and Darlugdach at Abernethy. The additional paragraph makes no reference to chronology at all (and in that respect alone is quite unlike anything else in the *Pictish Chronicle*) and, after noting the details of the grant of land, tells of the meeting between Nechtan and St Brigid (with no mention of Kildare or

Darlugdach). The two documents, with their quite different contents, blend together perfectly. Within a short time of gaining the throne, Nechtan must have sent word to St Brigid at Kildare. Within a couple of years Darlugdach was on her way to receive the gift of Abernethy on her behalf. She was the natural choice for such a mission, being St Brigid's favourite pupil and her eventual successor as the second Abbess of Kildare.

Nechtan was an exile in a foreign country with none of the cares of office to occupy his mind. In such a situation the new religion must have been just what he needed: not only something totally fascinating in its own right, something to learn, something to do; but also holding out a hope for the future, a ray of light at the end of the long, dark tunnel of exile. And Nechtan was not alone in being attracted to Christianity in such circumstances. Lindisfarne (Holy Island in Northumberland), one of the greatest Christian foundations in the whole of Britain, had its origin in exactly the same way. During the reign of Edwin of Northumbria, who died in 633, his nephews, Oswy, Eanfrid and Oswald, lived in exile among the Picts and Scots. While there, all three became Christians and were baptized. Eanfrid married a Pictish princess and was the father of Talorgan, who became King of the Picts. Oswald returned home and became King of Northumbria, whereupon he immediately sent to Iona for a bishop to instruct his people in the Christian faith. Aidan was sent in answer to this request, and Oswald granted him the island of Lindisfarne.[22] Nechtan, like Oswald, probably attributed his success in attaining the throne to his new-found Christian God and, like Oswald, gave land for the foundation of a church, both to show his gratitude and to bring the new religion to his people.

The first recorded Christian mission from Ireland to the Picts, based at Abernethy and commencing in about 485, came by invitation following Nechtan's return from exile and his accession to the throne. The circumstances of his exile are not related, but are not difficult to imagine. The long reign of Drust son of Erp was dragging on, with the old king probably becoming increasingly incapable but refusing to hand over to a younger man. What little we know about the Pictish system of succession may have worked very well when choosing a successor to a deceased king, but made no provision for pensioning off a king who had seen better days. The same is of course true of other monarchies with the 'standard' patrilineal system of succession. Two solutions for this problem have been devised: regency and palace revolution. In the Pictish system there was no recognized heir to the throne, just a number of well-known candidates from whom the next king would be chosen when the time arose. As a reign moved towards its natural end through old age, the supporters of the chief candidates would be preparing for the coming election. Nechtan must have been seen as a strong candidate to follow Drust, but the old king refused to die. As time went on the situation became desperate and he decided to make a bid for power. But the attempt failed (perhaps this was seen as the last of Drust's many battles) and Nechtan was exiled.

The only problem with the story of Drust and Nechtan is the statement that Nechtan was banished to Ireland by his brother Drust. There are many instances in the *Pictish Chronicle* of kings being succeeded by their brothers, presumably by virtue of descent from the same royal mother. But if Drust really had an extraordinarily long reign and was followed by Talore son of Aniel who reigned for 4 years and then Nechtan himself who reigned for 24 years, it is biologically impossible that he and Nechtan could have had the same mother. It is just possible that they could have had the same father, but this would not in itself have made Nechtan a candidate for the throne. It is perhaps more likely that they were not brothers at all and that this relationship was added much later, owing to the similarity of their fathers' names. Drust's father is variously recorded as Erp, Ws, Irb and Yrb, whereas Nechtan's father is Erip, Wirp or Eirip. The idea of Nechtan being unjustly exiled by his cruel brother also adds a suitable element of hardship to the early life of the king who was responsible for introducing Christianity to his people.

Drust died in about 478, after a reign memorable for its length and for the number of battles fought. We cannot be sure just when he came to the throne, but a long reign implies a long life, and we may be able to form some opinion as to what constituted a long life in those days. Three score years and ten is a familiar biblical notion of our natural lifespan, and a long life might have been one that exceeded 70 years. St Columba died in 595 in his seventy-sixth year, and St Adomnan in 704 in his seventieth year. St Patrick lived for about 72 years and St Brigid for about 82. To achieve a notoriously long reign, Drust probably lived well into his seventies and would thus have been born at about the beginning of the fifth century.

If a prophet had foretold a life of many battles for Drust, he could not have chosen a better birth date for him. The last vestige of the Roman army in Britain was withdrawn in 407 by the western Emperor Constantine III who, like Magnus Maximus before him, marched on Italy in a vain attempt to bring the whole empire under his control. He was defeated and executed in 411, and the legions never returned to Britain. There were some in Britain who saw their hope in a return of Roman authority and, to that end, appeals were sent to Emperor Honorius in 410 and Emperor Aetius in about 446. There were others, like Vortigern, who realized that this was a lost cause and decided to take control of their own destiny and that of their country.[23] It was a time of confusion in southern Britain, but nonetheless a time when the material wealth accumulated during the years of Roman occupation was still very much in evidence. Southern Britain was an ideal target for raiders and invaders, and the Picts, Scots and Saxons were already familiar with the country. That was the situation in Britain when Drust son of Erp was King of the Picts.

In one well-known battle in 429, the Britons faced a combined force of Picts and Saxons. We know about this particular battle because the Britons fought under the leadership of St Germanus, Bishop of Auxerre, and the event was recorded in an account of his life written no more than 50 years later. Details of the battle, though unfortunately with no indication of where it took place, were also included in Bede's *Ecclesiastical History of the English People*.[24] St Germanus, who was in Britain to combat the Pelagian heresy, took command of the disheartened and untrained British troops. As the enemy approached, the whole army shouted 'Alleluia' three times until the surrounding hills echoed with the great battle cry. The enemy were so astonished that they took to their heels and fled. That is one side of the story anyway. The Pictish version has not survived. It is quite possible that Drust fought in this 'Alleluya battle' as a young man, and he must have fought in many others when the Britons did not have a bishop to lead them to victory. He may also have fought against the Saxons, when these were first called into service as federates by Vortigern. For a Pictish king with an appetite for warfare, the fifth century was a period rich in opportunity.

CHAPTER 10

The Spoils of War: the Fifth Century

The many battles of Drust son of Erp in the fifth century were different from those fought by his predecessors against the Roman legions. In those earlier centuries the young Pictish nation had been fighting for its survival against what must have seemed a very real threat of foreign domination. By Drust's time that threat had been removed. The last of the legions had crossed the sea to Gaul, and southern Britain, far from being a threat to the Picts, lay fat and defenceless before them. Raids on southern Britain, which in the fourth century might have been construed as legitimate attacks on enemy territory, had degenerated into marauding expeditions, the sole object of which was plunder. The Picts (and the Scots) had become the Vikings of the fifth century.

It is fortunate that some trace of these expeditions has been preserved in the archeological record. The ideal loot from these raids would have had to combine maximum value with minimum bulk, for ease of transport on the homeward journey. Cattle, for example, though valuable, would have been out of the question for a raid involving a journey of several hundred miles by sea. Silver came very close to the ideal and, though finds of Roman and Pictish silver are by no means common, they make up for their rarity by their richness and significance.

The best known find of Roman silver in Britain is the Mildenhall treasure from Suffolk, which was ploughed up in 1942. This hoard consists of a wonderful collection of dishes, bowls, cups and spoons, ranging from a great circular dish, over 2 feet (60 cm) in diameter and weighing more than 18 lb (20 kg), decorated with Bacchanalian figures and sea nymphs swarming round the central bearded head of the god Neptune, to spoons bearing the Christian chi-rho monogram set between the Greek letters alpha and omega. Much of the silver was imported from Gaul or the Mediterranean, and it dates possibly from the third century to as late as the middle of the fourth century. It was buried to save it from being plundered by some enemy, very likely Pictish or Scottish raiders. Exactly when it was concealed we do not know; it could have been any time after the middle of the fourth century. The owner never returned to recover his property and its secret died with him, hidden not only from the enemy but also from his rightful heirs. That is the British side of the story. Many hoards of silver must have been hidden

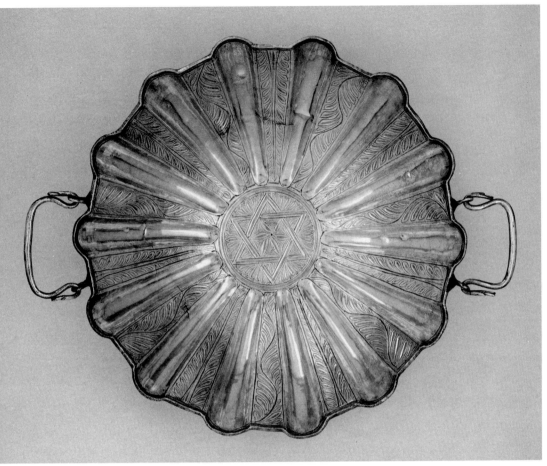

Fluted silver bowl from the Mildenhall (Suffolk) treasure (Photo: British Museum).

away in this manner and most of them recovered when the danger had passed. But much of this wealth must have passed into enemy hands, either through misfortune or through lack of foresight on the part of the owners.

The greatest hoard of Roman silver in Scotland was discovered on Traprain Law in East Lothian, during excavations inside the great hillfort in 1919. Like the Mildenhall treasure, it contained Christian spoons, and also coins of the Emperor Honorius (395–423). Unlike the Mildenhall treasure, much of the silver had been crushed or broken up for melting down. The most natural interpretation of the Traprain Law hoard of Roman silver is that it was loot resulting from a Pictish raid (or raids) on southern Britain. But Traprain Law is south of the Firth of Forth and therefore beyond the generally accepted southern boundary of Pictland. Furthermore the hillfort on Traprain Law is generally recognized as the stronghold of the *Votadini*, a tribe which seems to have enjoyed good relations with the Romano-British government during the late fourth and early fifth

Fluted silver bowl from the Traprain Law (East Lothian) treasure (Photo: National Museums of Scotland).

centuries. Why should Pictish loot have been buried in such an unlikely place? These difficulties seem so serious that one authority has stated 'it is unthinkable that the Traprain treasure is loot, and it is most easily interpreted as a payment in bullion either to secure friendly relations, or to pay for the services of Votadinian mercenaries'.[1] And, quite apart from these problems, who was threatening the occupants of Traprain Law to such an extent that they buried their hoard of silver and never returned to collect it? Some consideration must be given to these matters before we proceed any further.

There is no documentary evidence for the location of the southern boundary of Pictland in the fifth century, or of the northern boundary for that matter. As far as the written record goes, there is no reason why the whole of southern Scotland might not have been Pictish at this time. The evidence for the conventional boundaries of Pictland derives from a much later period. Traprain Law is one of the largest hillforts in the whole of Scotland and seems to have been the stronghold of the *Votadini*. Its origins go far back into prehistory, and it reached its maximum size in the first century AD, possibly just before the Roman invasion of Scotland. The defences were rebuilt several times in the next few centuries and then, finally, completely redesigned with a 12 feet (3.5 m) thick, stone-faced turf-cored wall in the late fourth century. There is little evidence of occupation beyond about the middle of the fifth century. Of particular interest in the present context is the latest period of occupation and its possible connection with the foundation story of the kingdom of Gwynedd in North Wales.

Above: square silver dish with beaded rim from Mileham, Norfolk (Photo: British Museum).
Below: square silver dish with beaded rim (fragments) from Traprain Law (Photo: National Museums of Scotland).

Above: dolphin-handled silver ladles from Mildenhall (Photo: British Museum). Below: dolphin-handled silver ladle from Traprain Law (Photo: National Museums of Scotland).

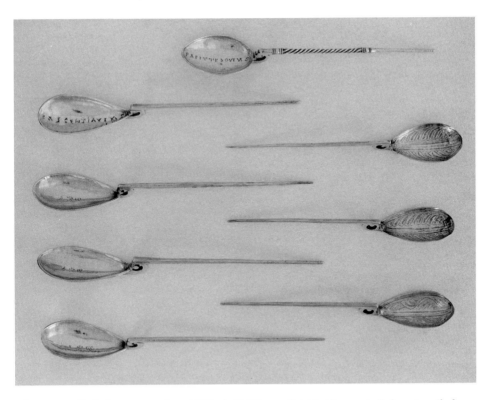

Above: inscribed silver spoons from Mildenhall (Photo: British Museum). Below: inscribed silver spoon from Traprain Law (Photo: National Museums of Scotland).

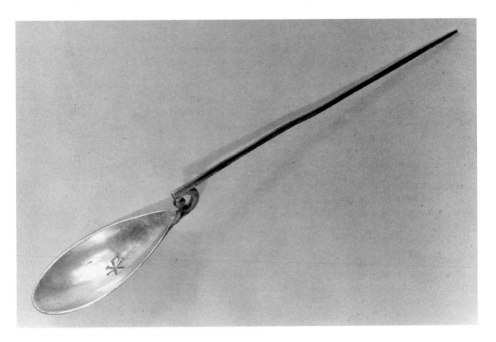

Crushed silver flasks from Traprain Law (Photo: National Museums of Scotland).

According to the tradition collected by Nennius in the ninth century,[2] Cunedda, ancestor of Maelgwn the Great, King of Gwynedd, came from Manau Gododdin with his eight sons and drove out the Irish (*Scotti*) from North Wales. These events are stated to have taken place 146 years before the reign of Maelgwn. Manau Gododdin, described as being in the north, is correlated in a general way with the territory of the *Votadini*. Further detail is given among the pedigrees assembled in the time of Hywel Dda, King of Wales (909–50). Here we learn that Cunedda had nine sons: Tybion, Ysfael, Rhufon, Dunod, Ceredig, Afloeg, Einion Yrth, Dogfael and Edern. Tybion, the eldest, stayed behind and died in Manau Goddodin, but his son, Meirion, joined the expedition and was responsible for dividing the newly acquired land with his uncles, the eight sons of Cunedda.[3] Most of these sons can be recognized in the names of counties or smaller districts in North and Central Wales: Meirionydd (Merioneth), Ceredigion (Cardigan), Rhufoniog, Edeirnion and others.[4] In the genealogy of Hywel Dda, Maelgwn is shown as the grandson of Eniaun Girt, son of Cunedda. The whole story has a distinct resemblance to the legend of the seven sons of Cruithne and the origin of the Picts, but has nonetheless been taken seriously by many historians.[5]

Cunedda's expedition, whether it was undertaken as a result of deliberate (Roman) government policy (the most widely held view) or whether it was an unsolicited migration, had two major results in North Wales: the expulsion of the Irish and the permanent settlement of his own people. The effects in his home

Traprain Law, stronghold of the Votadini: oblique aerial view from the west (Photo: Cambridge University Air Photographs).

country must have been no less far reaching. The removal of such an effective fighting force from Manau Gododdin must have created a military vacuum. For the Picts, this would have presented an ideal opportunity to control the whole of the Firth of Forth and thereby provide a safer passage for their marauding fleets. Both the archeological and the historical dating are far too imprecise to enable us to say whether the final reconstruction of the Traprain Law hillfort took place before or after Cunedda's departure for North Wales. It must, however, be admitted as a possibility that the final occupation of Traprain Law may have been Pictish rather than Votadinian, a possibility which makes it much easier to understand the great hoard of silver as Pictish loot from raids on southern Britain. There remains the question of its burial. Like the Mildenhall treasure, it was presumably buried at a time of danger and never recovered. What was that danger?

A well-known tradition, collected by Nennius and, independently, by Geoffrey of Monmouth, lists the battles attributed to Arthur, which culminated in the great victory at Mount Badon.[6] The battle of Mount Badon, fought at the beginning of the sixth century, led to several decades of peace. Most of the battles appear to have been fought against the Saxons, but there is one, mentioned by both Nennius and Geoffrey, that was fought in the Caledonian wood and must almost certainly have been against the Picts. No one can tell just where this battle was fought, except that it was somewhere in Scotland. An attack on southern Scotland by a British army could well have been the occasion for the concealment of the Traprain Law treasure and, if the battle resulted in the defeat of the Picts, the permanent loss of the treasure until it was rediscovered in the twentieth century would also be explained.

The hoard of silver from Norrie's Law in Fife provides the next link in the story. This was found in a gravel pit early in the nineteenth century and most of it was unfortunately melted down by a local jeweller before it could be properly recorded. Much of it, like the Traprain Law treasure, was cut up and crushed ready for melting down. The surviving objects include the twisted fragment of an inscribed Roman spoon of fourth-century date[7] and two fourth-century Roman

Broken and twisted bowl of inscribed silver spoon from Norrie's Law, Fife (Photo: National Museums of Scotland).

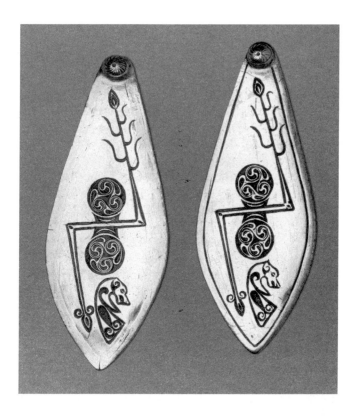

Silver plaques with Pictish symbols from Norrie's Law (Photo: National Museums of Scotland).

silver coins. The great interest of this hoard is that, unlike the Traprain Law hoard, it also contained examples of Pictish silverwork. The best known of these are two remarkable leaf-shaped plaques, each beautifully inscribed with a pair of symbols, a double disc and Z-rod, and a seal's head. Found in historical Pictland and inscribed with Pictish symbols, there can be no doubt about the 'nationality' of these objects. The date of the Norrie's Law hoard has been a matter of some debate. The surviving Roman artefacts and silver coins indicate that it cannot be earlier than the late fourth century. Three large hand-pins, one of which is engraved with a Z-rod on the back of the pin-head, are very similar to hand-pins from a late Roman context in southern Britain. There is nothing in the hoard to suggest that it belongs to a period later than the fifth century.[8] Why was it buried and not recovered?

The presence in the same hoard of a large amount of scrap silver, ready for melting down, together with a smaller number of finished objects of Pictish origin, suggests that the hoard was the stock in trade of a working silversmith. For such a man, every day presented the danger of potential loss of the store of silver, which was his livelihood. He could not carry it round with him as he travelled about the country visiting his clients; it would have been too heavy and he would have been far too vulnerable. He would have had to hide it in a safe place whenever he went abroad, though he might have left an apprentice or a member of his family in charge. But even in times of peace, things can go wrong. Perhaps the silversmith of Norrie's Law had no one he could (or would) trust with the knowledge of his safe hiding place. It was safer, though perhaps less profitable, to work in the protected environment of a hillfort, such as Clatchard Craig, also in Fife, where clay moulds for casting silver pin-heads and brooches have been found,[9] but no hidden hoards of silver have been discovered. The Norrie's Law silversmith preferred to work alone and, when he failed to return one day, the secret of his hoard died with him.

The symbols engraved on the Norrie's Law plaques lead us on to another class of silver objects: the massive silver chains, one of which is similarly engraved. The chains, weighing 2 to 3 kg, are made up of double circular links, and the ends could be joined by means of a terminal 'napkin ring' so that they could be worn as necklets on ceremonial occasions. Ten of these chains have been found, mostly in southern Scotland, beyond the limits of historical Pictland, including one on Traprain Law. One of these, from Whitecleugh near Crawfordjohn in Lanarkshire, has Pictish symbols engraved near the open ends of the terminal ring. One of the symbols is a double disc and Z-rod, so like those on the Norrie's Law plaques that it might even have been engraved by the same artist. The other symbol is a geometrical design which is less well known, but is also represented on a symbol stone at Falkland in Fife. There seems little doubt that these silver chains are Pictish, but why are the majority of them found outside Pictland to the south?

It has been suggested that the silver chains found in southern Scotland might have been looted from the Picts by the Northumbrians during their northward expansion in the seventh century. That would have been just retribution for all the silver stolen by the Picts in earlier times, and no one seems to have come up with a better answer. But the Picts left their unmistakable mark in the south, not only on portable silver chains, but also on a solid rock outcrop near the entrance to a hillfort. The site is Trusty's Hill at Anwoth, near Gatehouse of Fleet in Galloway, with a view across the Solway Firth to the south. The symbols are a double disc and Z-rod, a sea beast, and a unique circular insect head with long curved antennae. These cannot be interpreted as loot captured from beleaguered Picts by the advancing Northumbrians.

The symbols carved on solid rock on Trusty's Hill must surely represent a statement of ownership, and A.C. Thomas, who carried out an excavation there in 1960, suggested that the hill had been captured by Pictish raiders.[10] If the Picts were able to take a fortified hilltop so far from their own country, what else must they have achieved? There is just one thing that provides a link all the way from Norrie's Law in Pictish Fife, through the silver chains spread right across southern Scotland, to Trusty's Hill on the Solway Firth, and that is a Pictish symbol: the double disc and Z-rod. If only we could read the meaning of that symbol.

Unlike the Egyptians, the Picts did not write long hieroglyphic texts, and the symbols most frequently occur in pairs. Each symbol must therefore have represented a whole word, or perhaps a name or a concept. Deciphering the Egyptian hieroglyphics followed the discovery of the Rosetta Stone on which

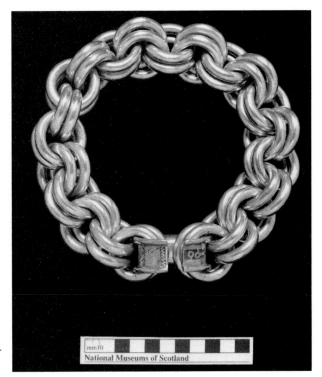

Massive silver chain with Pictish symbols from Whitecleugh, Lanarkshire (Photo: National Museums of Scotland).

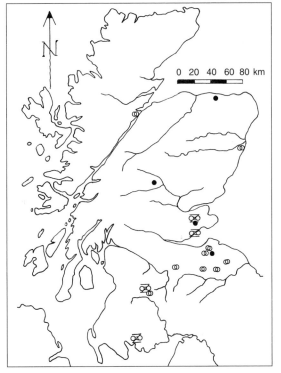

Distribution of silver chains (linked circles), hoards of silver (black dots), and incised 'double disc and Z-rod' symbols on silver, on rock outcrops, and on cave walls in mainland Scotland.

Trusty's Hill (Dumfries and Galloway). Left: looking eastwards across the ramparts from the entrance (Pictish symbols carved on a rock outcrop are protected by an iron cage, which makes photography almost impossible); right: sea beast and dagger symbols on a rock outcrop near the entrance to the fort.

three versions of the same text were inscribed, one in hieroglyphics, one in Egyptian demotic characters and one in Greek. For the Pictish symbols the nearest approach to a Rosetta Stone is the Drosten Stone, in the collection of Pictish stones at St Vigeans near Arbroath. This is a cross slab, the back of which displays Pictish symbols in the midst of an amazing collection of wild animals. Near the base of one side of the stone is a roughly square panel, about half filled by three and a half lines of writing – possibly an unfinished inscription. The top line of the inscription is the name Drosten, and the upper symbol is a double disc and Z-rod. Drosten is a variant of the name Drust or Drest, known elsewhere as Tristan, and recognizable in Trusty's Hill.[11] Could these be the symbols of Drust son of Erp, the fifth-century King of the Picts who became a legend (if not in his own time, not many decades later) for his long reign and his many battles.

The double disc and Z-rod is the common factor in the symbol pairs discussed above, but the symbols which accompany them vary from place to place. Thus they cannot be read simply as Drust son of Erp. But, if we look at near contemporary Latin inscriptions of this form, such as *Drustanus filius Cunomori* on a stone near Fowey in Cornwall, the reason immediately becomes clear. Such inscriptions are generally found on memorials to the dead.

Above: double disc and Z-rod symbol on a rock outcrop near the entrance to the fort on Trusty's Hill. Below: insect's head symbol on a rock outcrop near the entrance to the fort on Trusty's Hill.

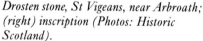

Drosten stone, St Vigeans, near Arbroath;
(right) inscription (Photos: Historic
Scotland).

The symbols on the rock outcrop on Trusty's Hill would be better compared with Latin inscriptions set up over the entrance to great public buildings, such as the Forum at Verulamium.[12] This records, in the top two lines of the inscription, the name and titles of the Roman Emperor Titus, followed in slightly smaller lettering by the name and titles of his younger brother Domitian. Finally, below these imperial authorities, we come to their local representative, Agricola, the Governor of Roman Britain. The inscription thus gives a hierarchy of authority. Taking this as a model, the symbols on Trusty's Hill could be interpreted as follows: double disc and Z-rod for Drust, King of all the provinces of the Picts; sea beast for the name of some long-forgotten local king of Galloway; insect's head perhaps for the officer in command of the fort itself. The same interpretation could be applied to the symbols of the Whitecleugh silver chain. This was probably the chain of office of the local king and displayed his own symbol together with that of the high king, Drust. In considering the symbols on the Norrie's Law plaques, it may be significant that the same pair of symbols was carved on the wall of a cave at East Wemyss only 7½ miles (12 km) away to the south-west, though there is no direct evidence for the date of this carving.

In summary, then, the legendary figure of Drust son of Erp, who reigned for a hundred years and fought a hundred battles, should be allowed to take his rightful place as a major character in the history of Britain in the fifth century. Early in his career he probably took part in the conquest of much of southern Scotland. Then, from safe harbours, he organized and led marauding expeditions to southern Britain. One of these harbours was in Fleet Bay, overlooked by the hillfort still known as Trusty's Hill.

Later in his long reign, as he grew old and less capable of maintaining the unity of his great kingdom, he began to suffer not only from dynastic troubles but also from enemy attacks, culminating in a great defeat remembered by the victorious British as the battle of the Caledonian wood, which effectively brought the period of Pictish rule over southern Scotland to an end.

This period of Pictish rule over southern Scotland in the fifth century has no part in the accepted history of Scotland. There is no documentary evidence for it, either contemporary or later, but no more is there any documentary evidence at all for the extent of the Pictish kingdom at this time. It is therefore put forward here as a working hypothesis, which not only fits the available historical sources, but also provides a consistent explanation for several archaeological anomalies, in particular:

1   the hoard of looted Roman silver found on Traprain Law;
2   the relative abundance of Pictish silver chains in southern Scotland;
3   the Pictish symbols carved on a rock outcrop on Trusty's Hill.

In this context too it is little wonder that many of St Ninian's converts to Christianity reverted to their old ways. This is also the setting for the letter of St Patrick to Coroticus, whose soldiers had apparently been selling Irish Christians as slaves to the 'utterly evil and apostate Picts'.[13]

Author's note Since this book went to press I have read N.J. Higham's recent book on Gildas and the English conquest of Britain, and been reminded that Gildas (an almost contemporary authority) did indeed record just such a conquest of southern Scotland as I have suggested in this chapter. He said that 'they [the Picts and the Scots] seized the whole of the extreme north of the island from its inhabitants, right up to the wall'. Gildas had probably never met a Pict or a Scot, and his statement that 'they were readier to cover their villainous faces with hair than their private parts and neighbouring regions with clothes' seems to owe more to Dio Cassius ('they dwell in tents, naked and unshod, and possess their women in common') than to contemporary observation. But this is no reason to doubt his statement about the conquest of southern Scotland, particularly if, as Higham argued, he was writing far away in lowland Britain, south of the Thames.[14]

CHAPTER 11

Into History: the Sixth Century

Brude son of Maelchon, King of the Picts, reigned for 30 years, and in the eighth year of his reign was baptized by St Columba. He is the third and last of the kings about whom the *Pictish Chronicle*, in its original form, has anything to say apart from the length of his reign. That this event was of more than passing interest is shown by its inclusion in Bede's *Ecclesiastical History of the English People*, according to which:

1   Columba came over from Ireland 'to preach the word of God to the northern Picts';
2   he arrived in the ninth year of the reign of 'the powerful Pictish king, Brude son of Maelchon';
3   he converted the people by his preaching and example;
4   he received from the Picts the island of Iona for the foundation of a monastery;
5   his disciples went out and founded many more monasteries.[1]

At first sight there is a curious inconsistency between Bede's writing and the *Pictish Chronicle*. Bede said that Columba arrived in Britain in the ninth year of the reign of Brude, but the *Pictish Chronicle* recorded Brude's baptism by Columba as being in the eighth year of his reign. Either source might have made an error in the regnal year, or Brude might have been baptized in Ireland before Columba set sail for Britain. According to the Irish annals, Columba sailed from Ireland in 563 and Brude son of Maelchon died in 584.[2] If he reigned for 30 years, as stated in the *Pictish Chronicle*, he must have come to the throne in 553 or 554. The eighth year of his reign will therefore have begun in 560 or 561 and ended in 561 or 562, at least a year before Columba left Ireland. The Irish annals are, however, perfectly consistent with Bede's statement that Columba arrived in Britain in the ninth year of Brude's reign. They also give one further piece of information about Columba's arrival: that Conall son of Comgall (King of the Dalriadan Scots) granted the island of Iona to Coluimcille (Columba). This contrasts with Bede's statement that Columba received the island from the Picts.

From the brief statements in the *Pictish Chronicle*, in the Irish annals, and in Bede's *Ecclesiastical History of the English People*, it is clear that there are several questions to be answered. Did Brude cross over to Ireland to be baptized? Did Columba come over from Ireland on a mission to convert the northern Picts? Who really granted him the island of Iona? Why was Brude's baptism of such importance that it is recorded in all versions of the *Pictish Chronicle*? To attempt an answer to any of these questions, we need to know more about the two principal characters in the story: Brude son of Maelchon, the King of the Picts, and Columba, the founder and first Abbot of Iona.

Of Brude we have very little detailed information. Bede described him as a powerful Pictish king. In the year 560, according to the Irish annals, he put the Dalriadan Scots (Albanich) to flight. Some years later, according to Adomnan's *Life of St Columba*, he was holding hostages of the King of Orkney.[3] These two facts imply military activity on two different fronts, one somewhere to the west of the spine of Britain and the other beyond the northernmost point of mainland Britain. Scanty the facts may be, but they are in complete accord with Bede's description of Brude as a powerful king.

Of Columba we know a good deal more, largely owing to the fact that his life was written up, within a few generations of his death, by two of his successors in the abbey of Iona, Cumaine ailbe and Adomnan. Of these two lives, Cumaine's only survives in a passage quoted by Adomnan, and Adomnan's has surprisingly little to say about any missionary work among the Picts. The first thing to understand about Adomnan's *Life of St Columba* is that it is not a biography in the modern sense, with the principal events of his life arranged and discussed in chronological order, but a collection of more or less isolated incidents, selected to illustrate his miraculous powers. The text is arranged in three books, the first of which deals with 'prophetic revelations', the second with 'miracles of power', such as healing the sick, and the third with apparitions, either of angels or of 'heavenly light', sometimes seen by Columba and sometimes seen around him by others.

The incidents recounted in Adomnan's *Life of St Columba* are of considerable interest in themselves, but for the historian their value lies in the incidental details of their circumstances, the names of the people involved, and where they were and what they were doing at the time. A few examples will suffice to illustrate the point. One day Columba was sitting in his hut when he heard someone shouting across the water that separates Iona from Mull. He turned to his attendant, Diormit, and said that the man who was making all the noise would upset and spill his ink horn. Sure enough, in a little while, the visitor arrived and rushed in to greet the saint, and in his haste knocked over the ink horn with the edge of his garment.[4] On another occasion one of the monks, Colcu son of Cellach, was studying in the hut. Columba, who was sitting with him, suddenly said to him, 'Now demons are dragging to hell one grasping leader from among the chief men of your district.' Colcu immediately made a note of the date and hour on a tablet, and when he returned home a few months later he learned that Gallan son of Fachtne had died 'in the same hour in which the blessed man had told him of the seizure by demons'.[5]

It was not Adomnan's intention to tell his readers about Columba and his monks reading, writing and studying in their huts on Iona; that would have been common knowledge. The stories themselves are about prophecies made and fulfilled, and we may, if we wish, question their veracity. The incidental details, however, provide reliable information about the life and times of Columba simply because they are incidental. Many of the stories related by Adomnan have a domestic setting on Iona, similar to those outlined above, and it is fairly clear that Columba must have spent much of his time at home on his little island, carrying out the administrative and pastoral duties of an abbot, studying the scriptures, teaching the younger members of his community, receiving and accommodating visitors, and so on.

There are just two stories in Adomnan's *Life of St Columba* which relate to his conversion of the Picts east of the spine of Britain. In the first of these Columba was preaching among the Picts through an interpreter, when a certain unnamed man 'believed the word of life' and was baptized, together with his wife, children and servants. A few days later his son was taken ill and was at the point of death. The pagan magicians of the Picts were delighted at this failure of the Christian's God. By the time Columba heard the news the boy was already dead. He encouraged the parents to have faith in the power of God and went to kneel alone and pray by the body of their son. After a while he got up from his knees and addressed the boy, 'In the name of the Lord Jesus Christ be restored to life, and stand upon thy feet', whereupon the boy opened his eyes. Columba took him by the hand, raised him up and led him out of the house. The assembled people let out a great shout of joy and 'the God of the Christians was glorified'.[6] We are not told how many more of the Picts were converted as a result of this miracle – the story is about the miracle of healing, not about the conversion of the Picts.

On another occasion, when Columba was on a journey across the spine of Britain, he was walking along the shore of Loch Ness. Suddenly he had a vision of holy angels descending to conduct the soul of a pagan and waiting for him to be baptized, because he had 'preserved natural goodness through his whole life, into extreme old age'. Columba, by this time himself described as 'the aged saint', dashed off ahead of his companions and came to the farm called Airchartdan (Urquhart). There he found the dying man, Emchath, his son Virolec and his whole household. He preached the word of God, and they believed and were all baptized. Emchath then gladly 'departed to the Lord', with the angels who had come to meet him.[7] Once again the story is not primarily about the conversion of a whole household of Picts, but about the vision of angels, which led Columba to their dwelling.

Whatever we may think about the miracles, it is quite clear from these stories that Columba's day-to-day business in the land of the Picts was preaching the word of God, converting them to Christianity and baptizing them in complete family units or households. This brings us, as Smyth has said, 'to one of the greatest enigmas surrounding Columba's life, namely the extent of his involvement with the Picts and the justification for the claim that he was the Apostle of Pictland'.[8] How many expeditions he made across the spine of Britain in the course of his missionary activity we cannot tell. The reference to his 'first tiring expedition to king Brude' implies that he visited him on at least two occasions, and the statement that thereafter, 'throughout the rest of his life, that ruler greatly honoured the holy and venerable man'[9] seems to suggest that they met on a fairly regular basis.

If we were to take Adomnan's *Life of St Columba* as a guide to the proportion of time he spent in different places and on different activities, we would have to conclude that he devoted most of his life, after leaving Ireland, to his monastic duties as Abbot of Iona. But Adomnan himself shows us why we cannot use the life in that way. He points out in his introduction that he has been most careful to include only the most authentic material, passed on by trustworthy men or already set down in writing.[10] His readiest sources of such reliable information would have been the library and the older brethren in the abbey of Iona itself. In other words Adomnan's attempt to include only the best material immediately leads to a bias in favour of incidents which took place on Iona and an under-representation of stories from faraway Pictland. In this connection the last of Columba's miracles related by Adomnan is of interest. It was a posthumous miracle and took place in Adomnan's own time. On two occasions, when the rest of Europe was ravaged by plague, only the Picts and the Scots of northern Britain remained free of it. Adomnan attributed this miraculous escape to Columba, 'whose monasteries, placed within the boundaries of both peoples, are down to the present time held in great honour by both'.[11] The foundation of these monasteries by Columba is not recorded elsewhere by Adomnan, not because such foundations did not take place, but because they were not accompanied by well-authenticated prophecies or miracles.

Adomnan does not record the baptism of King Brude by Columba, but we cannot conclude from this, as Smyth has done,[12] that Brude did not become a Christian. The statement in the *Pictish Chronicle* that Brude was baptized by Columba in the eighth year of his reign must mean not only that he did become a Christian, but also that his baptism was, for some reason, a matter of the greatest (national) importance. Fortunately, Adomnan does give an account of Columba's first visit to Brude's fortress by the River Ness.[13] Brude, we are told, 'uplifted with royal pride, acted haughtily, and did not open the gate of his fortress at the first arrival of the blessed man'. So Columba went up to the gate, made the sign of the cross on it and knocked, and the doors were miraculously opened for him. When the king heard of this he was 'much alarmed . . . and went to meet the blessed man with reverence; and addressed him very pleasantly, with words of peace'. The story is about the miraculous opening of the barred gates, and Adomnan told it from the point of view of Columba's missionary party. It is worth looking at it in some detail.

The actual events, as the missionary party experienced them, can be summarized as follows:

1   they reach the fortress and find the gate barred against them;
2   Columba performs his miracle of opening the gates;
3   the king appears and gives them a friendly welcome.

The statement about the king's royal pride and haughty action is a literary explanation for the gate being barred. It is most unlikely that Columba or anyone else would have asked the king why the gates were locked, and even more unlikely that such an explanation would have been forthcoming. Brude was a powerful king, of that we can be in no doubt. Such a man might well have barred the gates of his fortress against foreign intruders, whatever their mission, but if those intruders had then proceeded to force the gates, he would have been justifiably angry. To come and meet their leader with reverence and with words of peace would have been completely out of character. So what is the explanation of these events?

The opening and closing of the fortress gates would hardly have been the personal responsibility of the king. It would much more likely have been delegated to the captain of the guard or some such officer, in which case we no longer need to seek an explanation for the king's sudden change in attitude from haughty to reverential. But why, if he did not already know Columba, would he have treated a representative of a strange religion with such reverence? He was on his own home territory, where his power was absolute. What right had these foreign priests to come breaking into his stronghold? It doesn't make sense, unless Brude had already met Columba before his first tiring journey across the spine of Britain, and unless he had been baptized by Columba in the eighth year of his reign, the year before Columba left Ireland for a permanent 'exile' on Iona. But why was Brude so keen to become a Christian? The reason may be found in the circumstances of his rise to power.

Nechtan son of Erip, the first Christian king of the Picts, died in about 506. He was succeeded by Drust Gurthinmoch, who reigned for 30 years, and then by Galanan erilich, who ruled for a further 12. Then, in about 548, the 'electorate' failed to reach a decision between the two main contenders for the throne, and the Picts found themselves under the joint leadership of two kings, Drust son of Girom and Drust son of Wdrost; probably with the intention that when one of them died, the survivor should continue to rule over the whole kingdom. In the event, Drust son of Wdrost was the first to go, but Drust son of Girom failed to unite the whole kingdom behind him and Brude son of Maelchon was elected king in succession to Drust son of Wdrost.[14] We now have, for the first time, the situation implied by Bede: a Pictish nation split geographically into southern and northern parts, the southern Picts being Christian and the northern Picts pagan.

Brude had probably from an early age been destined for high office and had been brought up in the household of the magician (*magus*) Broichan, who is referred to by Adomnan as his foster father.[15] The word *magus* is sometimes translated as 'druid', and probably in the case of Broichan means nothing less than high priest. Not only was Brude a pagan, but it seems that he was quite deliberately given a highly conservative education, steeped in the traditions and practices of the old religion. It looks as if he was being prepared as a bulwark against the creeping Christianity of the south.

Drust son of Girom died, but the southern Picts would have nothing to do with the pagan king of the north. They chose Drust's brother Gartnait as their king, apparently happy to let the Pictish nation remain divided. This religious divide between the two Pictish nations could easily have resulted in a permanent separation, had it not been for the ambition and determination of one man, Brude son of Maelchon, and he wanted to be king of all the provinces of the Picts, as his predecessors had been. It was becoming clear that the southern Picts were unshakeable in their adherence to the new Christian God. Politically the solution was obvious: if the southern Picts would not revert to the old religion, the northern Picts must be converted to the new one. And, in spite of his upbringing, this was exactly the plan that Brude decided to adopt.

In the year 560, when Gartnait son of Girom had been King of the southern Picts for about 2 years, the Irish annals made their first reference to Pictish affairs with the statement that Brude son of Maelchon, King of the Picts, put the Scots to flight. The location of this battle is not given, but Brude's most likely line of advance would have been down the Great Glen, the exact reverse of Columba's journeys across the spine of Britain. A victory in this direction would have given him access to the Firth of Lorne and a good sea passage to northern Ireland, and that was just where he needed to go to find out more about the God of the Christians.

Two years later, in the eighth year of his reign, he was baptized by Columba. It seems that, at about this time, Columba had committed (or was alleged to have committed) some offence and was under sentence of excommunication by an Irish synod.[16] It may well be that Brude, following his victory over the Scots, was able to offer him the island of Iona in exchange for a promise of missionary work among the northern Picts. This would have been an offer hard to resist, quite apart from his problem with the synod. Remote island retreats were much sought after by the early Irish saints, and Columba's friend Cormac, grandson of Lethan, made three hazardous journeys in search of a 'desert in the ocean'.[17] If this is the correct interpretation of the records, Columba accepted the offer with enthusiasm and, a year later, left Ireland on the mission which was to put him at the top of the league among Scotland's many saints.

As Columba's mission to the northern Picts got under way, the southern Picts continued to pursue their separatist policy. Garthnait son of Girom died and was succeeded by a third brother, Cailtram, who reigned for only a year. He was succeeded by Talorgan son of Muircholaich, and he in turn by Drust son of Munait, who died in about 578. By this time Brude had been King of the northern Picts for 24 years, and for 15 of those he had ruled as a declared Christian and his people had received the benefits of Columba's missionary activity. The new king of the southern Picts, Galam cennaleph, was a much younger man, and a generation had passed since the first acrimonious split between the Christian south and the pagan north. According to the *Pictish Chronicle*, he ruled for a year by himself and another jointly with Brude son of Maelchon. The Irish annalists recorded his death in the year 580, the first Pictish king to have his passing noted in this way. That is all we know about him, but his short reign was of vital importance.

Brude probably called on Galam cennaleph, not long after he came to the throne in southern Pictland, and set out his plan for a reunited kingdom of the Picts. The plan was a simple one, namely that the two kings should rule together over the united kingdom until one or the other died, whereupon the survivor would carry on by himself. On his death the next king of all the Picts should be chosen in the time-honoured way from the female royal line. For the young King Galam, this must have seemed like a promise of greater power to come in the not too distant future. For Brude, who may have proposed the same plan several times before, it must by this time have been as much for the good of the nation as to satisfy his own personal ambition. The treaty was signed and the joint rule began. Within the year, Galam cennaleph was dead and, against all the odds, Brude son of Maelchon was undisputed king of all the provinces of the Picts. The key to his success was a policy decision, made early in his reign, to adopt the Christian religion himself and then to promote the conversion of his people to the faith. The turning point in his career was his baptism by St Columba in the eighth year of his reign and, in a sense, that same baptism was a turning point also in Columba's career.

CHAPTER 12

Northumbrian Neighbours: the Seventh Century

The English kingdom of Northumbria came into existence in about the year 605, under the leadership of Ethelfrid, described by Bede as 'a very powerful and ambitious king' who 'ravaged the Britons more cruelly than all other English leaders'.[1] At the beginning of the century, Ethelfrid was King of Bernicia, the northernmost of the English kingdoms, centred on the great coastal fortress of Bamburgh. In about 603 (600 in the Irish annals) he defeated a considerable army under the leadership of Aedan mac Gabran, King of the Dalriadan Scots. Degsastan, the site of this battle, has never been satisfactorily located. Having thus dealt with the threat from the north, he turned on his own kinsman, Edwin of Deira, whose kingdom occupied much of Yorkshire. Edwin lost his kingdom but escaped with his life. Bernicia and Deira were united to form the powerful new kingdom of Northumbria, though the differences between them continued to influence the history of the north for many decades.

Edwin wandered from place to place, with Ethelfrid's agents never far behind, trying to secure his assassination. Eventually he found an ally in Redwald, King of the East Angles and probable owner of the Sutton Hoo treasure. They assembled an army and marched northwards. Ethelfrid, taken by surprise and greatly outnumbered, was defeated and killed. Edwin of Deira, after years of exile, became King of Northumbria in 617.[2] Now the boot was on the other foot and the three sons of Ethelfrid were sent into exile, together with many other young nobles. Eanfrid, the eldest, Oswald, aged about thirteen, and Oswy, only about five, were to spend the next 17 years among the Picts and Scots. This period of exile was to have far-reaching repercussions.

Edwin brought Northumbria into a position of pre-eminence among the English kingdoms. On the death of his friend Redwald, King of East Anglia, he was accepted as *bretwalda*, or overlord, by the other English kings in Britain. His reign was noted for its law and order, to such an extent that Bede was able to write, a hundred years later, 'that the proverb still runs that a woman could carry her newborn babe across the island from sea to sea without any fear of harm'.[3] In the end, the Mercians, under Penda, and the Welsh, under Cadwallon, formed an alliance against him and the two armies met at Hatfield, near Doncaster, on

12 October 633. Edwin was killed and his entire army destroyed, and Bede gave a graphic description of the ensuing devastation of Northumbria.[4]

During Edwin's reign, his exiled kinsmen had been growing up among the Picts and Scots, learning their languages and absorbing their culture. All three brothers were converted to Christianity and baptized during their exile, and fell, to a greater or lesser extent, under the spell of Iona. Eanfrid, who was either adult or nearly adult at the time of his exile, may have been less impressionable than his younger brothers, but took the politically important step of marrying into the Pictish royal family. We do not know the name of his wife, but she belonged to the exclusive female royal line and bore him a son, Talorgan, who was to become King of the Picts, thus ensuring a family connection with the kings of Northumbria.

During the confused period following Edwin's death, Eanfrid tried in vain to regain his father's kingdom of Bernicia, while Edwin's cousin Osric made a similar attempt in Deira. Within the year both were dead, Osric killed in battle and Eanfrid treacherously slain while trying to negotiate peace. The whole of Northumbria groaned under the tyrannous rule of the Welsh king Cadwallon. Where Eanfrid had failed, his brother Oswald succeeded. Marching southwards through Bernicia, he met and destroyed Cadwallon's army just north of Hadrian's Wall, a few miles from Hexham. He quickly established himself as king over the whole of Northumbria and, like his uncle Edwin, was recognized by most of the other English kings as *bretwalda*. The Mercians, however, continued to resist this Northumbrian supremacy and, in 642, Oswald was slain in a fierce battle against Penda of Mercia. Oswald was succeeded in turn by his younger brother, Oswy, who reigned over Northumbria and held the position of *bretwalda* until his death in 670. He too was harassed by the Mercians during the first half of his reign, but he finally defeated them in 655.

Northumbria, during much of the seventh century the most powerful of all the English kingdoms, was looming large on the Pictish horizon. Picts and Northumbrians could view each other's territories across the eastern end of the Firth of Forth. What was the relationship between the two kingdoms? According to Bede, himself a Northumbrian, Oswald 'brought under his sceptre all the peoples and provinces of Britain speaking the four languages, British, Pictish, Irish and English',[5] and Oswy 'subjected most of the Picts to English rule'.[6] Taken at face value, these statements seem improbable in the extreme, particularly in view of the difficulties both kings experienced from Mercia.

However the Northumbrians achieved their alleged supremacy over the Picts and Scots, it seems to have been a remarkably bloodless affair. The only battles mentioned by Bede are those already noted above against the Mercians and their allies, and these same battles were also recorded by the Irish annalists. If these annalists recorded Northumbrian battles against the faraway Mercians, how much more would they have noted such conflicts in the land of the Picts?

The battles recorded by the annalists are probably only a small selection of the many actually fought. Bede, for example, wrote that 'Oswy was subjected to savage and intolerable attacks by Penda the . . . King of the Mercians', but the only battle he mentions as such was the decisive encounter in which Penda was defeated and lost his life.[7] Warfare was endemic, and battles were noted by the annalists only if they seemed at the time to have some special significance, such as the death of a king or a change in the political geography.

Five Pictish kings are recorded by the Irish annalists as having died during the reigns of Oswald and Oswy, Kings of Northumbria: the three brothers, Garnard, Brude and Talore, sons of Wid (Foith), Talorgan son of Enfret, and Gartnait son of Donnel. Of these, Talorgan was certainly a nephew of the two Northumbrian kings, and the others were probably close relations by marriage. None of them is noted as having been slain in battle, whether at the hands of the Northumbrians or anyone else. Battles were recorded, but none between the Northumbrians and the Picts. The only military engagement recorded by the Irish annalists in this period, which might have involved the Northumbrians, is the siege of Edinburgh in 638. This was the last stronghold of the British *Votadini*, the base from which those ill-fated heroes, immortalized by the British poet Aneurin in *Y Gododdin*, had marched southwards and met their death storming the old Roman fort at Catterick.[8]

If there is any truth in Bede's statements about Oswald and Oswy subjecting the Picts to their rule, and there seems no good reason to doubt them, this cannot have been the result of military conquest. The only other possibility is that the Pictish kings joined the majority of the English kings in recognizing Oswald and Oswy as bretwaldas over most of Britain. Such recognition would probably have involved the payment of tribute.[9] So what was in it for the Picts? Kings of powerful nations do not acknowledge neighbouring kings as their overlords, tribute or no tribute, unless there is some political or military advantage to be gained from such action. To find the answer, we must look back to the beginning of Oswald's reign.

After defeating Cadwallon and restoring order to his devastated kingdom, Oswald's main concern was to establish the Christian religion on a firm footing throughout Northumbria. He therefore sent to Iona for a bishop to whom he could entrust this important mission. Aidan, 'a man of outstanding gentleness, holiness and moderation',[10] arrived in answer to this call, and Oswald granted him the tidal island of Lindisfarne. History was repeating itself. Seventy years after Columba set up the base camp for his mission on the little western island of Iona, Aidan was carrying that same mission right across the country and establishing his own base on an even smaller island off the Northumbrian coast. Nothing could be a more telling indication of the success of Columba's own mission than this direct extension of his work.

Aidan had little command of the English language, and the Northumbrians knew no Gaelic. So keen was the king to see the success of Aidan's mission that he himself often acted as an interpreter for his new bishop. Irish monks arrived in considerable numbers and settled throughout Northumbria, and the king granted land for the establishment of their monasteries. When Aidan died, a new bishop, Finan, was sent over from Iona, and he in turn was succeeded by Colman, another Iona monk.

Oswald and Oswy may have acquired some form of temporal overlordship over the Picts and Scots, but this was more than balanced by a spiritual overlordship in the opposite direction. There cannot be the slightest doubt that Oswald and Oswy acknowledged the spiritual overlordship of the Abbey of Iona, and this was something of incalculable value to the Iona-based Christian kingdoms of the Picts and the Scots. Iona had become for Northumbria what Rome was to be for most of western Europe during the Middle Ages. There seems little justification for viewing any of the Pictish kings in this period as Northumbrian puppets.[11] The admittedly scanty evidence seems rather to suggest that there was a special relationship between the Northumbrian kings and the Picts and Scots among whom they grew up. Whatever the truth about Anglo–Pictish relations at this time, the seeds of change had already been sown.

Oswy, probably not long after he came to the throne, made a politically sound marriage to his cousin Eanfled, daughter of Edwin of Northumbria, thus cementing the link between the two parts of Northumbria, Edwin's Deira and his own Bernicia. Oswy's new queen was a young girl of some 17 years and, like her husband, she had spent much of her young life in exile. She was a Christian and her mother, Ethelberga, was daughter of Edwin, the King of Kent who had welcomed St Augustine's mission and 'granted them a dwelling place in the city of Canterbury'.[12] This was in 597, about a generation after St Columba began his mission to the Picts. When Ethelberga married the then pagan King Edwin of Northumbria, she was accompanied on her northward journey by Paulinus, a Roman priest who had been sent by Pope Gregory to assist St Augustine. Paulinus became Bishop of York, and one of his duties was to preserve the queen and her companions 'from corruption by their association with the heathen'.[13] When Edwin was killed and Northumbria overrun by Cadwallon, Paulinus deemed it advisable to escape and sailed for Kent with Queen Ethelberga, her daughter Eanfled and other members of the royal family.

Oswy and Eanfled were both Christians, but their Christianity came from opposite ends of the world – Oswy's from Ireland via Iona and Eanfled's from Rome via Kent. These two branches of the Christian church, now meeting in the middle ground of Northumbria, had been evolving separately for more than two centuries, and there were differences between them which could not easily be overlooked. To begin with the clergy looked different. Just as today a Church of Scotland minister preaching his sermon looks different from a Roman Catholic priest celebrating mass, so in the seventh century Irish monks looked different from Kentish monks. The most obvious difference between them was the form of the tonsure. The Irish monks had the front of their heads shaved, back to a halfway line between the ears, whereas the Kentish monks had the whole top of their heads shaved, leaving only a circular fringe of hair. The importance of this tonsure may be judged by the story Bede related about Theodore of Tarsus, who was appointed Archbishop of Canterbury in 668 at the already advanced age of 66. Up till that time Theodore had worn the eastern tonsure, which was different again, so he had to delay his journey to England for four months while his hair grew, so that he could receive the circular tonsure of the Roman church.[14]

The difference in tonsure might just have been tolerated, had it not been for a more fundamental difference between the two churches in the calculation of the date of Easter. Working out the proper date for Easter was, and is, by no means a simple matter. When Nechtan, King of the Picts, wrote to Ceolfrid, Abbot of

Wearmouth and Jarrow, asking for guidance on the timing of Easter, the reply was an essay of some three thousand words, followed by another thousand on the correct form of the tonsure and the reasons behind it.[15] Now that these two Christian traditions were met together, not only in the same country but also in the same family, something had to be done to resolve the problem. In some years the Roman and Celtic Easters fell on the same day, while in others they were a week apart. As Bede wrote, there were years when the king, guided by his Irish bishop, was celebrating Easter while the queen and her household, advised by her Kentish priest, were still fasting and keeping Palm Sunday.[16]

A synod was convened and the participants assembled at Whitby in the year 664. King Oswy opened the proceedings and then his own bishop, Colman, spoke for the Celtic church. He was followed by Wilfrid, Abbot of Ripon, who put the Roman case. It was not long before the debate became acrimonious, and Wilfrid is reported as having said, 'the only people who stupidly contend against the whole world are those Irishmen and their partners in obstinacy the Picts and the Britons, who inhabit only a portion of these the two uttermost islands of the ocean'.[17] While these may not have been Wilfrid's exact words, the sentiments expressed do seem to fit the views of the Roman faction. Bede himself never missed an opportunity to point out the errors of the Celtic church. Thus, after giving a glowing account of the life and work of St Aidan, he had to spoil it all by adding: 'but I cannot approve or commend his failure to observe Easter at the proper time, whether he did it through ignorance of the canonical times or in deference to the customs of his own people'.[18] King Oswy made the closing speech and declared his wholehearted support for the Roman church. The supremacy of Iona over the Church in the north of England, which had lasted a mere 30 years, was gone for ever.

After the synod, Bishop Colman returned disillusioned to Iona, carrying with him some of the bones of his predecessor, St Aidan. Many of the Irish clergy followed him, as well as some thirty English monks who had been taught by him. A few years later he sailed for Ireland and founded a monastery on Inishboffin, a small island off the west coast, where he died in 676. Oswy began to play his part on the international scene and entered into correspondence with the Pope about the appointment of the next Archbishop of Canterbury. He and Egbert, King of Kent, sent their candidate, an English priest called Wighard, to Rome, with presents for the Pope, including many gold and silver vessels. The Pope wrote back 'To our son, the most excellent Lord Oswy, King of the Saxons', thanking him for the presents, but regretting that Wighard had died while in Rome. He sent relics of the Apostles Peter and Paul, and of the martyrs Laurence, John, Paul, Gregory and Pancras, for the king, together with a cross made from the fetters of the Apostles Peter and Paul, with a golden key, for the queen. The Pope closed his letter with the hope that Oswy would soon 'dedicate your whole island to Christ our God'.[19]

The Synod of Whitby may have brought an unprecedented degree of unity to the Christian church in England, but it also resulted in a sharp religious as well as political divide between the Picts and Scots 'north of the border' and the Northumbrian English south of it. The Picts and Scots were drawn together under the religious umbrella of Iona, while the Northumbrians joined the rest of England and turned their faces to Rome. As far as we know from the limited historical sources, the border remained quiet until the death of Oswy in 670. Then two things happened which must surely have been related. The expulsion of Drust son of Donnel from the kingdom of the Picts is recorded in the Irish annals the year after the death of Oswy, and his death is noted 6 years later.[20] Then, from south of the border, Eddius Stephanus in his life of Wilfrid gave an account of a major victory of the Northumbrians over the Picts, early in the reign of Ecgfrith, son and successor of Oswy.

Eddius Stephanus did not say where the battle was fought, nor in which year, but he leaves us in no doubt at all as to why it was fought. The Picts came swarming down from the hills of the north, determined to free themselves for ever from 'subjection to the Saxons'. In the ensuing battle the Picts suffered a terrible slaughter, and it is said that two rivers were filled with their dead, to the extent that the Northumbrians were able to cross over dry-shod on their bodies and pursue the fugitives from the battle. The tribes of the Picts were once again 'reduced to slavery and remained subject under the yoke of captivity'.[21] Not long after this, Ecgfrith met and defeated a similar 'uprising' under the leadership of Wulfhere, King of the Mercians, and here we have specific reference to the payment of 'tribute in a slavish spirit', and after the battle the Mercian kingdom was 'laid under tribute'.[22] By close analogy it seems clear that the 'slavery' of the Picts involved the payment of tribute to the Northumbrian king as their overlord.

Drust son of Donnel was expelled from the kingdom. But was he a Northumbrian puppet, expelled by his own people when Oswy died, as supposed by Smyth;[23] was he a true Pictish king, expelled by his own people when his stand against the Northumbrians failed, as supposed by Anderson;[24] or was he expelled from his kingdom by the Northumbrian army? We cannot know. How much Pictish territory came under direct Northumbrian rule as a result of this battle is by no means clear, but it is quite unrealistic to think of all the tribes of the Picts being in this state.

As Ecgfrith extended his authority northwards across the land of the Picts and southwards over Mercia, Bishop Wilfrid extended his spiritual jurisdiction.[25] Ordaining priests and deacons to help him in his work, he tirelessly pursued his mission of establishing the Roman Catholic church as the 'state religion'. Ecgfrith and Wilfrid made a powerful team, but it was not to last. Wilfrid had a taste for pomp and ceremony, a love of power, a desire to show his importance by the size of his retinue, and a taste for worldly wealth (even though this was ostensibly for the payment of his clergy and the upkeep of his churches). The queen drew the king's attention to Wilfrid's behaviour, and together they consulted the Archbishop of Canterbury and decided to remove Wilfrid from his high office.[26] Wilfrid's vast see was split up into more manageable units, the most northerly and probably most challenging of which was given to Trumwine, who was 'to be bishop of those Picts who were then subject to English rule'.[27] It is perhaps an indication of the political climate of the times that Trumwine chose the monastery of Abercorn, safely situated on the southern shore of the Firth of Forth, as the centre of his see.

As the years went by, Ecgfrith seems to have become dissatisfied with the situation in the north. English overlordship, even over the occupied territories, seems to have been somewhat superficial, and the progress of the Roman church had been minimal. In 685, against the advice of all his friends, Ecgfrith decided that the time had come for action. He assembled an army and marched northwards into the land of the Picts. He crossed the Forth and the Tay without event. The Picts watched the progress of the invading army and waited their opportunity. This came at last on 20 May, when the Northumbrian army found itself trapped in a great marshy area known as Nechtansmere, overlooked by the Picts on the hills around Dunnichen, a few miles east of Forfar. In the ensuing battle, Ecgfrith was killed and most of his army destroyed. The battle of Nechtansmere must rank alongside Bannockburn as one of the most decisive in the history of Scotland. Not only did the Picts regain control of the land formerly occupied by the Northumbrians, but the Dalriadan Scots and the Strathclyde Britons regained their freedom from English overlordship. The effect of this great Pictish victory was even felt south of the Firth of Forth. Bishop Trumwine and all his people were forced to withdraw from the monastery of Abercorn and take refuge further south.[28]

Brude son of Bile, the victor of Nechtansmere, died in 693 and was succeeded by Taran son of Entifidich, but for some reason he did not come up to expectation. He was expelled 4 years later and took refuge in Ireland. He may have been found guilty of softness towards the Northumbrians, because in 698, early in the reign of his successor, Brude son of Derile, there was yet another battle between the Picts and Northumbrians, in which the Northumbrian leader, Bertred son of Bernith, was killed.[29] Neither Bede nor the Irish annalists recorded the site of this battle, but it must have been another Pictish victory, thus consolidating the gains made at Nechtansmere.

CHAPTER 13

The Struggle for Power: the Eighth Century

The eighth century opened well for the Picts. Following the victory at Nechtansmere, the burden of English overlordship had been removed, not only from the Picts, but also from their neighbours the Dalriadan Scots and the Strathclyde Britons. So far as we can tell from the limited evidence, all the provinces of the Picts were under one rule. At the turn of the century, Brude son of Derile was king, and when he died, in 706, his brother Nechtan succeeded him. The Picts and the Scots were drawn together, with their religious life centred on the mother church of Iona and the cult of St Columba.

Not long after his accession, Nechtan decided that he had a Christian mission in life, in addition to his royal duties. He had made a study of the Easter controversy and had come to the conclusion that, in this respect at least, the Roman church had the right answer. He therefore wrote to Ceolfrid, Abbot of Wearmouth and Jarrow, asking for details so that he could introduce the Roman system with authority. He also requested further information on the correct form of tonsure for his clergy, and asked for architects to be sent so that he could build a stone church in the Roman style. Ceolfrid's detailed reply, which was reported in full by Bede, was exactly what Nechtan required. He immediately sent out a decree to the churches throughout all the provinces of the Picts, requiring them to adopt the new Roman system for computing the date of Easter and instructing the clergy to have their hair cut according to the circular (Roman-style) tonsure.[1] The year was 711. Five years later, and quite independently of Nechtan's action, the monks of Iona also changed over to the Roman system for calculating the date of Easter.[2] Superficially, this looks like a significant move towards church unity across the whole country, and this is certainly how Bede saw it. And yet in 717, the very next year, Nechtan expelled the 'family of Iona' across the spine of Britain. What possible reason could there have been for this high-handed action?

Thanks to Bede's interest we know more about Nechtan son of Derile than almost any other Pictish king. As Bede said rather smugly, he 'asked help from the English people, whom he knew to have based their practice long previously on the pattern of the holy Roman apostolic Church'. And when Ceolfrid's letter was delivered, he was so delighted that he is said to have fallen on his knees in front of

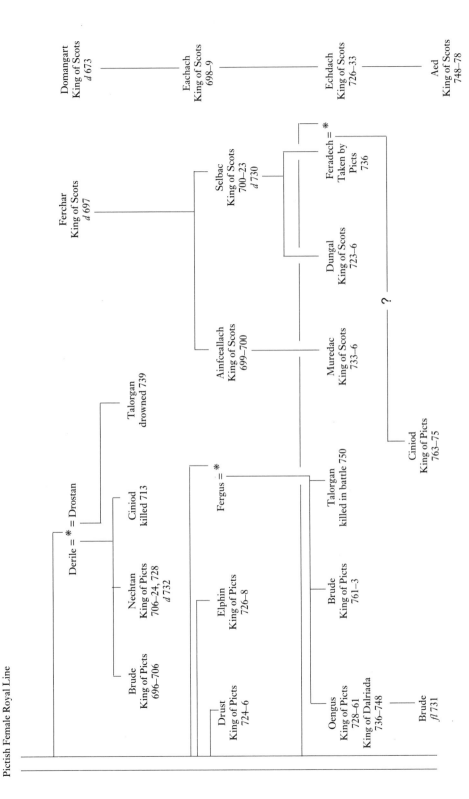

Pictish Female Royal Line

Domangart
King of Scots
d 673

Eachach
King of Scots
698–9

Echdach
King of Scots
726–33

Aed
King of Scots
748–78

Ferchar
King of Scots
d 697

Selbac
King of Scots
700–23
d 730

Feradech =⁕
Taken by
Picts
736

Dungal
King of Scots
723–6

Ainfceallach
King of Scots
699–700

Muredac
King of Scots
733–6

?

Derile =⁕ = Drostan

Talorgan
drowned 739

Ciniod
killed 713

Nechtan
King of Picts
706–24, 728
d 732

Brude
King of Picts
696–706

Fergus =⁕

Elphin
King of Picts
726–8

Talorgan
killed in battle 750

Ciniod
King of Picts
763–75

Drust
King of Picts
724–6

Brude
King of Picts
761–3

Oengus
King of Picts
728–61
King of Dalriada
736–748

Brude
fl 731

Genealogical tables of the Pictish and Scottish kings to illustrate the struggle for power in the first half of the eighth century.

his assembled chieftains and thanked God 'that he had been accounted worthy to receive such a gift from England'. It is quite clear that Bede looked on Nechtan as an enlightened anglophile Pict. It is probable that many of Nechtan's Pictish contemporaries put exactly the same interpretation on his dealings with the Northumbrians, and viewed him as a treacherous and potentially disastrous anglophile king. The problem now was political rather than religious; but what happened in 717 to tip the balance?

Dunchadh son of Cindfaeladh, the Abbot of Iona who had presided over the change from the Celtic to the Roman Easter in 716, died in the following year, while the change and its political implications were still fresh in the minds of the people. Kings, princes and nobles, as well as monks and priests, would have had an interest in the political leanings of his successor. The question at issue was no longer the date of Easter – that had been settled once and for all. What mattered now was whether the Church, and the State with which it was increasingly entwined, was going to lean towards Rome or retain its traditional western orientation. Any further move towards Rome would inevitably have been seen as a move towards England. On the other hand, a conservative vote to retain Iona as the mother church of the Picts and Scots might have been seen as an anti-Roman backlash. Nechtan, according to Bede, had promised 'that he and his people would follow the customs of the holy apostolic Roman church, as far as they could learn them in view of their remoteness from the Roman people and from Roman speech'. His action in 717 suggests that the Iona-based clergy were not coming up to his expectations in this respect.

At the time of his accession, Nechtan had two surviving brothers, Ciniod son of Derile and Tolargg (Talorgan) son of Drostan. Talorgan was presumably a half-brother, a son of his mother's second marriage. The first sign of trouble in Nechtan's reign was the murder of Ciniod in 713, 2 years after the adoption of the Roman Easter. In the same year, Nechtan had Talorgan imprisoned. The statements in the Irish annals are brief in the extreme, but it is likely that Talorgan was suspected of complicity in his brother's death. Ciniod would have been the most likely heir in the event of Nechtan's death, and it may be that Talorgan, equally well descended from the female royal line, had ambitions for the throne, and felt a need to eliminate his strongest potential rival. He may also have tried to stir up an anti-Roman faction against the king, to support him in his own climb to power.

The suggestion that Nechtan was a weak king, whose overtures to Northumbria and Rome in 711 were politically motivated,[3] is not borne out by the facts of his reign. He maintained the unity of his great kingdom for nearly 20 years, and the fact that a period of civil war followed so closely on his departure is surely an indication of just how important his own personal qualities of leadership must have been. But in 724, Nechtan decided it was time to hand over to a younger man, while he retired to end his days in the Church.[4] The next king was simply called Drust, with neither the Irish annals nor the *Pictish Chronicle* ever referring to the name of his father. It was not long before Nechtan had cause to regret his retirement, and in 726 he must have tried to stage a comeback, because in that year he was put into prison by Drust. But Drust's own position was far from stable and, later in the same year, he was ousted by Elpin, who took over the kingdom.

The civil war proper began in 728, with the appearance of a strong new claimant to the throne. In 728 Oengus son of Fergus challenged Elpin at the battle of Monidcroib, generally identified as Moncreiffe, near Perth. Elpin's son and many of his followers were killed, and the victorious Oengus became king. Meanwhile, in all the turmoil, the old king, Nechtan, no longer under lock and key, assembled an army and set out to regain his kingdom. He met and defeated Elpin's army near Castle Credi and reclaimed the throne. Nechtan then set about the task of putting the kingdom in order and sent his tribute collectors out around the country. But he no longer had the popular support he had once enjoyed and, furthermore, he had not reckoned on the growing strength of Oengus. In 729 their two armies met at Monitcarno, which is sometimes identified with Cairn o'Mount, high up in the mountain pass which provided one of the essential links between the southern and northern Picts. Nechtan's army suffered a crushing defeat, and the death of his unwelcome tribute collectors attracted the particular attention of the Irish annalists. They included, among many others, Biceot son of Moneit, Finguine son of Drostan and Ferot son of Finguine. This battle was of such importance that it was even noted by the British (Welsh) annalists, the first of a small number of Pictish entries. In the same year Oengus came face to face with his one remaining rival, Drust, who had been Nechtan's nominee for the throne in 724. In this final battle of the civil war, fought at a place called Dromadarggblathmig, Drust met his death and Oengus became undisputed ruler of all the provinces of the Picts. Nechtan son of Derile died peacefully in 732.

The rapid turnover of kings during the civil war may have made very little impact on the bulk of the population, but it made things very difficult for the Pictish chroniclers in their task of recording the reign lengths of successive kings as an index of the passage of time. In the group A versions of the *Pictish Chronicle* the interval between Nechtan's retirement into the Church and his final defeat by Oengus is occupied by two kings, Drust and Elpin, who are said to have reigned together for 5 years. This apparent togetherness could hardly have been further from the truth, but the time interval is absolutely right. As a record of the passage of time, the chronicle serves its purpose well. As history it is less informative, but then it was never intended as a historical record. The group B versions of the *Pictish Chronicle* give a much better idea of the rapid succession of short reigns in this unsettled period, but are full of errors and inconsistencies.[5]

There is no way of telling whether this was a pseudo–religious war, between a Roman faction and an Iona faction, or whether it was simply a struggle for power between several claimants, each with an equal right to the throne by descent from the female royal line. What is certain is that, for a few years, the normal system of succession had broken down. In the end the country got what it needed: a strong king, tested on the field of battle. Anyone who challenged his authority was liable to death by drowning. In 734 Talorgan son of Drostan, possibly the Tolargg (Talorgan) son of Drostan who had been imprisoned by Nechtan 20 years earlier, was arrested and imprisoned. We are not told what he had done, but it seems that he represented a threat to the king, because in 739, now identified as King of Atholl, he was drowned by Oengus.

Success on the field of battle can easily become addictive, and, only a few years after the end of the civil war, Oengus was leading his armies westwards into the territory of the Dalriadan Scots. The trouble seems to have started in quite a small way in 731, with a battle between Brude son of Oengus son of Fergus and Talorgan son of Congus. Talorgan, whose father had a Scottish (Irish) name, may have had a Pictish mother, as his own name was certainly Pictish. He may even have been descended from the female royal line, and therefore potentially dangerous. Brude won the battle and Talorgan fled. Two years later Brude was captured by Dungal son of Selbac, who had been King of Dalriada until his expulsion in 726. Then, in 734, Talorgan was seized by his own brother and handed over to the Picts, who put him to death by drowning.

The Scots of Dalriada, like the Picts, had suffered a period of civil war, beginning in the mid-720s. In 723 Selbac, the old king who had reigned for more than 20 years, decided to retire into the Church and hand over to his son, Dungal. Dungal's reign lasted no more than 3 years before he was expelled by Echdach son of Eachach. Like Nechtan, Selbac emerged from retirement to do battle against the usurper, but he failed to restore order and died a few years later, in 730. The war dragged on, with no outstanding leader emerging to take control. In 731 Tairpirt Boittir, possibly Tarbert in Kintyre, was burned by Dungal, then in 733 Echdach died.[6] The contrast between the small leaderless kingdom of Dalriada and the much larger Pictish nation, united under its victorious king, Oengus son of Fergus, could hardly have been more striking. Oengus, with his family already involved in feuding in Dalriada, must have been well aware of the state of affairs. The Scots of Dalriada must have looked like a people just waiting to be conquered.

Oengus made his first attack on the Scots in 734, the year after the death of Echdach. He destroyed Dunleithfinn, the exact location of which has not been determined, and the wounded Dungal was forced to find refuge across the sea in Ireland (an eloquent testimony to the situation in Dalriada). In 736 Oengus struck again, laid waste to the land, captured the great fortress of Dunadd, north of Lochgilphead, and took Dungal (who had returned from Ireland) and his brother Feradech prisoner. Later that year Talorgan son of Fergus, the brother of Oengus, defeated a Dalriadan army and put the son of Ainfceallach to flight. This son must have been the Muredac son of Ainfceallach, who had assumed the kingship of Loairn, the northern part of Dalriada, in 733. In less than 10 years Oengus had made himself master of the whole of Scotland north of the Forth–Clyde line. His kingdom coincided broadly with the country known to the Romans as Caledonia, and this was the first time it had ever been united under the rule of a single king.

The Scots of Dalriada, however, managed to expunge this conquest from their national memory. Muredac is given a reign of 3 years in the *Duan Albanach*, consistent with the interval between the dates 733 and 736 noted above. He is followed by Aed, whose death as Aed son of Echdach, King of Dalriada, is recorded by the Irish annalists in 778. Aed is given a reign of 30 years and Oengus is not mentioned at all. The reign lengths recorded in the *Duan Albanach* are not noted for their accuracy, but if Aed did reign for 30 years, he must have come to the throne more than 10 years after the defeat of his predecessor, Muredac son of

Ainfceallach, by Oengus in 736. This gap may have been occupied by the unrecorded reign of Oengus over the Dalriadan Scots.

The rule of Oengus over Dalriada was not without its troubles, and in 741 he had to resort to force once again: '*Percussio Dalriatai*' by Oengus son of Fergus, as the Irish annalists recorded the event. He might well have been referred to, like Edward I of England, as the 'Hammer of the Scots', and in the long term his hammering was to prove no more effective than Edward's, but in 741 he was still winning.

The next recorded event in the long reign of Oengus was a battle between the Picts and the Britons in 750. This is the battle of Catohic of the Irish annals and was also recorded by the Britons as the battle of Mocetauc, which has been identified with Mugdock, between Milngavie and Strathblane, a few miles north of Glasgow. In this battle Talorgan son of Fergus, brother of Oengus, fell, and there was great slaughter of the Picts.[7] The Britons, in their record of the killing of Talorgan, thought that he was the King of the Picts. He may have been the local king of a part of Pictland or, perhaps more likely, he may have been in command of the Pictish army on this occasion, as he had been in the battle against the son of Ainfceallach in 736. Oengus continued to rule over the Picts until his death in 761, but after Mocetauc he was no longer the thrusting, expansionist, all-conquering king that he had been in the first half of his reign.

Oengus died in 761 and was succeeded by his brother Brude, who died 2 years later. Ciniod son of Wredech (Garnarde son of Feradhegh in the 1280 copy of the group B version of the *Pictish Chronicle*), the next king, may have been a son of Feradach son of Selbac, the Dalriadan prince taken prisoner by Oengus in 737.[8] But whatever the nationality of his father, Ciniod was a thoroughly Pictish king, and in 768 was defending his kingdom against an invading Dalriadan army. The Irish annals simply record a battle in Fortren between Aedh and Cinaedh. Aedh was the Aed finn son of Echdach, King of Dalriada, who died in 778. The fact that the battle took place in Fortren, one of the southern provinces of the Picts, suggests that the Scots had not forgotten their subjection by Oengus a generation earlier and were determined to retaliate. We do not know the outcome of the battle, but Ciniod (Cinaedh) died as King of the Picts in 775.

The first sign of renewed trouble among the Picts is the record in the Irish annals of the death of Dubhtolargg (Black Tolargg or Talorgan), described as King of the Picts 'this side of the Mounth' (*citra Monoth*). Dubhtolargg died in 782, but it is not immediately clear on which side of which mountain he had his kingdom. The Mounth usually refers to the range of mountains which extends eastwards from the spine of Britain and reaches down to the sea between Aberdeen and Stonehaven. This was the boundary between the northern and southern Picts, but the Irish annalists, whether they were writing in Iona or across the sea in Ireland, were viewing the Picts from the west. So who was this Black Talorgan, and who was ruling on the other side of the Mounth?

There are two possible candidates for the title of Black Talorgan in the *Pictish Chronicle*: Talorgan son of Drostan and Talorgan son of Onnist (Oengus). They appear in the sequence given below, with reign lengths from the chronicle and dates of death or defeat from the Irish annals.[9]

Brude son of Fergus (2 years)	died 763	(763)
Ciniod son of Wredech (12 years)	died 775	(775)
Elpin son of Wroid (3½ years)	died 780	(778)
Drust son of Talorgan (1 year)		(779)
Talorgan son of Drostan (4 or 5 years)		(782/783)
Talorgan son of Oengus (2½ or 12½ years)		(784/785)
Canaul son of Tarl'a (5 years)	defeated 789	(789)

If these kings really reigned in succession, there is not quite enough time available to accommodate all of the reign lengths. Working forwards from the death of Brude son of Fergus and backwards from the defeat of Canaul son of Tarl'a (dates shown in brackets), approximate dates for the deaths of the two Talorgans can be determined. On this basis it seems likely that Talorgan son of Drostan was the Black Talorgan, King of the Picts this side of the Mounth. The deaths of his immediate predecessor and successor were not recorded at all by the Irish annalists, noteworthy omissions in a sequence otherwise almost unbroken for more than 250 years. Perhaps they too ruled over a diminished kingdom and were not of sufficient importance to merit an obituary notice in the Irish annals.

The earliest version of the *Pictish Chronicle* was probably compiled at Abernethy, and a copy was made at Brechin towards the end of the tenth century. The group B versions of the *Pictish Chronicle* contain a number of references to the building of churches – at Abernethy, Dunkeld and Kilrymont (St Andrews) – and one copy refers to the arrival of St Servanus in Fife. All of these places are south of the Mounth and, since all versions of the chronicle list both Talorgans, it is fairly clear that 'this side of the Mounth' refers to the southern half of Pictland. It may also be significant that in the notice of the death of Elpin son of Wroid in 780, he is referred to as Elpin King of the Saxons. Was this an error, or is it possible that Elpin or one of his predecessors (perhaps the great Oengus) had conquered some of the Northumbrian territory south of the Forth?

The period of uncertainty ends with the reign of Constantine son of Fergus, one of the greatest Pictish kings. In 789 the Irish annalists record a battle among the Picts, in which Constantine defeated Conall son of Taidg (Canaul son of Tarl'a or Tang of the *Pictish Chronicle*). Constantine died in 820 and the group A version of the *Pictish Chronicle* gives him a reign of 35 years, which would take his accession back to the beginning of Conall's reign rather than the end of it, thus suggesting that he was already a king when he defeated Conall. In this connection it is interesting that Conall has no place in any of the group B copies of the chronicle, the implication being that he only ruled over part of southern Pictland, where his reign was recorded by the monks of Abernethy. Conall was probably a Scottish rather than a Pictish king, and may have come to rule over the western part of southern Pictland as the result of a battle like that between Aed and Ciniod in Fortren in 768. He was finally defeated and killed in Kintyre by Connal son of Aed in 807.

The reign of Constantine, given a length of 35 years by the group A version of the *Pictish Chronicle*, is variously recorded as 45 (1187 copy), 42 (1251 and 1317 copies) and 40 years (1280 copy) in the group B versions. These reign lengths would take his accession back to 775, 778 or 780, and suggest that he came to the throne in some part of Pictland, presumably north of the Mounth, on the death of Ciniod son of Wredech or Elpin son of Wroid, and that he was the King of the Picts 'on the other side of the Mounth' while Black Talorgan was ruling 'this side of the Mounth'. Whether Constantine increased his kingdom, like Oengus before him, by fighting and defeating his rivals, or whether he simply managed to take over when his rivals fortuitously died of natural causes, we have no means of knowing. From the middle of the eighth century the Irish annals provide only the sparsest details of Dalriadan and Pictish affairs. The 70 years from 680 to 750 fill seven pages of Skene's extracts from the *Annals of Ulster*, whereas the next 70 years to 820 occupy a mere two pages. Constantine's only recorded battle was the one in which he defeated Conall in 789.

Five years after Constantine's victory over Conall, a terse entry in the Irish annals recorded the devastation of all the islands of Britain by 'the gentiles'. A new external enemy had arrived on the scene – a voracious, barbaric and totally foreign enemy, a pagan enemy, an enemy to be resisted at all costs. The Vikings were to have a profound effect on the history of the Picts and the Scots.

CHAPTER 14

Kenneth mac Alpin, King of the Picts: the Ninth Century

The spine of Britain, which had been such a crucial factor in the separate development of the Picts and Scots, had been crossed and recrossed many times since St Columba's first historic journey. There was constant traffic between Iona and the Pictish church and, where the church gave the lead, the kings and their armies followed. By the end of the ninth century, whether at peace or at war, the Picts and the Scots were closer than they had been at any time since the Roman invasion. In contrast, communication across the Irish Sea, which had for centuries ensured the common cultural evolution of the Scots in Ireland and those in mainland Britain, had suddenly taken a turn for the worse. The natural perils of wind and weather, which could to some extent be avoided, were now augmented by the totally unpredictable danger posed by the Viking longships. The political geography of northern Britain had changed. The Scottish kingdom of Dalriada, now isolated from its parent across the sea in Ireland, clung precariously to the western seaboard, exposed alike to the familiar ravages of the Atlantic storms and to the new and terrifying onslaughts of the Viking raiders. In 806 Iona was attacked and the defenceless monks slain by the Vikings. The raiders probably returned home rejoicing, their ships laden with a rich haul of church silver. Such was the beginning of the ninth century for the Scots of Dalriada.

If we turn to the Irish annals to see how the Scots dealt with this new threat, we are in for a disappointment. After the death of Donncorci, King of Dalriada, in 792, the annals are silent on the subject. It is as if the Scots of Dalriada had ceased to exist. No more kings. No more battles. Nothing. Even Donncorci is a king of whom it has been said that we know nothing apart from the date of his death.[1] So what did become of the Scots of Dalriada? The king lists go some way towards providing the necessary continuity.

Aed finn son of Echdach, who died in 778, was followed by his brother Fergus, whose death was recorded in the Irish annals in 781. He was followed by Eochoid,[2] whose death passed unnoticed by the annalists. These two were followed by a series of kings, most of whom occur also in the *Pictish Chronicle*:

Scottish king lists	*Pictish Chronicle*
Domnall (mac Custantin) (24 years)	
Conall (Caeim) (2 years)	Canaul filius Tarl'a (5 years)
Conall (4 years)	
Cusantin (mac Fergus) (9 years)	Castantin filius Wrguist (35 years)
Aengus (mac Fergus) (9 years)	Unuist filius Wrguist (12 years)
Aodh (mac Boanta) (4 years)	
	Drest and Talorgen (3 years)
Eoganan (mac Aengus) (13 years)	Uven filius Unuist (3 years)
	Wrad filius Bargoit (3 years)
	Bred (1 year)
Cinaet mac Ailpin (30 years)	Cinaed filius Alpin (16 years)

The first thing to note in the Scottish list is that the fathers' names (shown in brackets) are not given in the shorter (and probably earlier) versions of the *Synchronisms of Flann Mainistreach*, nor do they appear in the *Duan Albanach*.[3] The Domnall at the head of the list has been confused with a Domnall mac Custantin who appears further down the list and was a grandson of Kenneth (Cinaed) mac Alpin. This mistake does not, however, affect the status of Domnall himself, though now of unknown parentage, and he may indeed be the Donncorci, King of Dalriada, who died in 792.

Some of the correlations shown above look a little less convincing than they really are, because of the difference between the Scottish and Pictish forms of some names. Thus Wrguist is the Pictish form of the Scottish Fergus; Unuist is equivalent to Aengus (Oengus); and Uven is the same as Eogan.

Following the death of Donncorci, though there is no further mention of Dalriada in the Irish annals, the kings listed above can still be recognized. In 807 Conall mac Taidg, the king who was defeated by Constantine in 789, was killed by Conall mac Aed. The second Conall, according to the *Duan Albanach*, reigned for 2 years and was followed by Custantin (Constantine), who reigned for 9. These reign lengths are just consistent with the death of Constantine son of Fergus in 820 (if, for example, the reigns were $2^3/_4$ and $9^3/_4$ years, totalling $12^1/_2$, and the death of Conall mac Taidg occurred in the second half of 807).

Constantine son of Fergus had a reign remarkable both for its length and its achievements. Some time before 782 he became King of the Picts north of the Mounth. On the death of Black Talorgan, in 782, he extended his power over most of the southern Picts. In 789 he defeated Conall mac Taedg in battle and extended his rule over all of the provinces of the Picts. On the death, defeat or resignation of Conall mac Aed in 809 or 810 (the event was not recorded by the Irish annalists), Constantine became King of the Scots of Dalriada as well, and ruled over them for the remaining 9 years of his life. His achievement was greater than that of his conquering predecessor, Oengus son of Fergus, because he was recognized as king by the Scots themselves. Exactly how he did it we may never know, but the menacing presence of the pagan Vikings was probably an important factor. A union of the Picts and Scots, if it could be sustained, made both military and political sense in the ninth century.

Constantine died in 820 as king of the combined kingdoms of the Picts and the Scots, and was succeeded by his brother Oengus. But what was their new kingdom to be called? It was more than Pictland, and to call themselves kings of the Picts might have seemed insulting to the Scots. It was also vastly greater than the old Scottish kingdom, so it would have been quite unrealistic to call themselves kings of Dalriada, and, as we have seen, that term went out with the death of Donncorci. Constantine and Oengus decided to style themselves kings of Fortren (at least this is how they were described when their deaths were recorded by the Irish annalists), and their armies then became the men of Fortren. This was a thoroughly diplomatic solution to the problem. Fortren, which may well have been the governmental centre of the new kingdom, was just one of the old provinces of the Picts and provided a name which carried no implication that either of the old kingdoms had been conquered by the other. Indeed the choice of Fortren as the name of the new kingdom might be taken to suggest that the union was indeed the result of diplomatic, rather than military, action.

The new kingdom of Fortren presented a united front to the outside world for about 20 years. Then, as the founders of the union grew old and died, ambitious younger men vied with one another for power and, inevitably, unity suffered as a consequence. How was the succession to be decided? The Scottish rule was essentially patrilinear, and the Pictish system matrilinear. There was no shortage of potential claimants, and four of these seem to have gathered enough support to make a serious bid for power. These were Aed mac Boanta, a Scot who set himself up against the dominant Pictish rule; Eoganan son of Oengus (King of Fortren); Drust son of Constantine (King of Fortren); and Talorgan son of Wthoil, presumably a traditional Pictish candidate descended from the female royal line.

Aed probably made his bid for power before the death of Oengus, whose reign in the Scottish king lists is 3 years shorter than in the *Pictish Chronicle*. Drust and Talorgan, on the other hand, may have waited till the old king died. The statement in the *Pictish Chronicle* that they reigned together probably means the exact opposite, though they may have reigned in different areas at the same time, north and south of the Mounth, for example. Eoganan seems to have waited to see how the situation would develop. He is the last of the four to appear, and the only one to have succeeded in reigning over the combined kingdom of the Picts and Scots. Furthermore, he seems to have ousted Aed mac Boanta without either killing him or incurring his undying hostility, as they both met their deaths fighting together against the Vikings.

The Vikings struck at the Picts and Scots in 839 in what was described by the Irish annalists as a battle between the Gentiles and the men of Fortren. There was great slaughter, and among the many dead were Eoganan son of Oengus, Bran son of Oengus and Aed son of Boanta. Eoganan is not named as King of Fortren, and it is quite possible that he had already been superseded by Ferat son of Bargoit, presumably another traditional Pictish claimant to the throne. A new leader was desperately needed: a man of the stature of Constantine; a man capable of reuniting his shattered kingdom. That man was Kenneth mac Alpin.

In all versions of the *Pictish Chronicle*, Kenneth reigned for 16 years, and the Irish annals record his death in 858. This would place his accession in 841 or 842, 2 or 3 years after the battle in which Eoganan and Aed lost their lives, but the Scottish king lists give no indication of any king between the death of Eoganan in that battle and the accession of Kenneth. For further details of the reign of Kenneth mac Alpin, we need to look at the final section of the 971–95 copy of the *Pictish Chronicle*, which is quite independent of the contemporary section of the standard group A chronicle and represents a genuine record of events, rather than a mere regnal chronology. This section closes with the statement that Kenneth son of Malcolm (who died in 995) granted the great city of Brechin to the lord,[4] and it may appropriately be referred to as the 'Brechin Chronicle'.

In the 'Brechin Chronicle' we read that Kenneth mac Alpin 'ruled Pictavia' for 16 years and that, before he came to Pictavia (*antequam veniret Pictaviam*), he held the kingdom of Dalriada for 2 years. There is no suggestion here that his arrival in Pictavia was anything other than peaceful and perfectly legitimate. The earlier statement about the Picts, 'who, as we said, Kenneth destroyed' (*quos, ut diximus, Cinadius delevit*), is clearly an editorial comment by the Brechin compiler, who felt it necessary to explain how the Picts of earlier times had been replaced by the Scots of his own time. It seems that Kenneth began his climb to power by establishing himself in Dalriada, in the aftermath of the Viking invasion. Then, reversing the order of Constantine's advance, he moved eastwards from his base in Dalriada, across the spine of Britain, and into the land of the Picts.

According to the group A versions of the *Pictish Chronicle*, Kenneth mac Alpin followed a king known simply as Bred, who had a short reign of only a year. The group B versions, however, are united in placing three more kings between Bred and Kenneth mac Alpin. Furthermore, though their opinion is divided as to whether Bred reigned for a year or only a month, all four copies are agreed on the reigns of the three extra kings. The information from the group B versions of the *Pictish Chronicle* may be summarized as follows, with an indication of spelling variation, where necessary.

Brude (Bred in group A) son of Ferat (Feradhach)	1 month/1 year
Kynat son of Ferat (Feradhach)	1 year
Brude son of Fotel	2 years
Drust son of Ferat (Feradhach)	3 years
Kynat (Kenneth) son of Alpin	16 years

The group B versions of the chronicle, which preserved some sort of record of the early phases of Constantine's rise to power, contain a similar record of the later phases of Kenneth's climb to an exactly comparable position. What these lists reveal is that there were independent Pictish kings, somewhere in the source area for the group B *Pictish Chronicle*, who between them resisted Kenneth's claim to the throne for 6 years. In other words, it took Kenneth mac Alpin a total of 8 years to reunite Dalriada and all the provinces of the Picts into the single kingdom that had been created under Constantine. Whether Kenneth's climb to power was achieved by diplomatic means or on the field of battle is not revealed in any of the contemporary sources. The Irish annals are silent on the matter.

The 'Brechin Chronicle'[5] contains a record of great activity in the seventh year of Kenneth's reign. Apart from transporting the relics of St Columba to a safe place in the church he had built, he invaded 'Saxonia' six times, burnt Dunbar to the ground and also captured Melrose. Other late sources, without giving dates, report that he extended his kingdom as far south as the Tweed.[6] Military activity in the seventh year of his reign seems to have been concentrated in the south-east of Scotland, south of the Forth, and yet this must also have been the year in which he overcame the last of the independent Pictish kings (the 6 years of their combined reigns would bring their end into the seventh year of Kenneth's reign). It seems likely that these kings ruled a Pictish province somewhere in the south-east, perhaps partly south of the Forth, a province which was finally absorbed into the main kingdom during Kenneth's advance in that direction. By the middle of the ninth century Kenneth mac Alpin was ruling over a kingdom greater even than Constantine's union of the Picts and the Scots, a kingdom that is clearly recognizable as the ancestor of medieval and modern Scotland.

Kenneth mac Alpin's death is recorded in the annals of his Irish and British neighbours, and both describe him as King of the Picts. He appears without comment in an unbroken sequence of kings in the standard (non-Brechin) group A *Pictish Chronicle*. He was quite clearly King of the Picts, and recognized as such by the Pictish chroniclers. Similarly his place in the early Scottish king lists assures us of his recognition by the Scots of Dalriada as their rightful king also. The next three kings, Donald son of Alpin, Constantine son of Kenneth and Aed son of Kenneth, were all described as kings of the Picts (*rex Pictorum*) in their obituary notices in the Irish annals. Thereafter a change takes place, and all subsequent kings are described as kings of Alba (*ri Albain*). The change looks, at first sight, much more significant than it is. All that really happened was that towards the end of the ninth century the language of the annals, which up to that time had been mainly Latin, changed to Irish (Gaelic). Whatever the old kingdom of the Picts had been called in the vernacular, the new enlarged kingdom was called Alba by the Irish, and since this name also persists in the Welsh language, there can be little reasonable doubt that it was in use by the Celtic peoples in general, including the Picts.

Kenneth mac Alpin was King of the Picts. He was also King of the Scots. Furthermore he was founder of the dynasty that has ruled Scotland in unbroken succession for well over a thousand years. But what was the basis for his authority? Did he rule by right of conquest or by right of inheritance, whether through the female royal line of the Picts or through the male royal line of the Scots, or did he base his power on some combination of these? Before attempting to answer these questions, we should appreciate that Kenneth was just one of ten known contenders for the throne during a period of some 15 years. Only one of these, Eoganan son of Oengus, had succeeded in extending his rule over the combined kingdoms of the Picts and Scots, and that only for 3 years. In Dalriada,

Aed son of Boanta had been ousted by Eoganan and then both had fallen in the disastrous battle against the Vikings in 839. In Pictland, Drust son of Constantine and Talorgan son of Wthoil had opposed one another and eventually been overcome by Eoganan, while he in turn had probably been pushed back into Dalriada by Ferat son of Bargoit.[7] On the death of Eoganan in the battle against the Vikings, there was, so to speak, a vacancy in the kingdom of Dalriada, whereas Ferat was still firmly in place as King of the Picts. Kenneth mac Alpin, who had probably fought in the battle, seized the opportunity and presented himself to the Scots as their king. These were desperate times and the prime qualities required of a new king were courage, resolve and leadership. Whatever his hereditary qualifications, Kenneth was in the right place at the right time, and now set about building a power base from which to extend his authority.

At first sight Kenneth mac Alpin looks like a typically Pictish claimant to the throne, as his father is quite unknown in either the early king lists or the Irish annals. But then we have to realize that the last King of Dalriada as such, the second of the two Conalls, must have died (or been defeated by Constantine) about 30 years before. Thus if Kenneth claimed descent through the male royal line of the Scots, we would expect his grandfather, rather than his father, to have been one of the known kings of Dalriada, and this is exactly what the later genealogies claim. Thus in the genealogy of William the Lion, dating from 1165, we read that Kenneth (Cinacha) was the son of Alpin, son of Echach, son of Aed (Eda-find), son of Echad.[8] According to this pedigree, Kenneth's paternal great grandfather was Aed finn, King of Dalriada, who died in 778 (the date of his grandfather's death is not recorded, though he too was a king of Dalriada). If this part of the genealogy is true, and there is no good reason to doubt it, then Kenneth's claim to the kingdom of Dalriada could not have been bettered.

Two years after claiming the throne in Dalriada, Kenneth succeeded Bred as king of most of the provinces of the Picts. If this was the result of conquest, and there is no contemporary evidence for it, it can only have been achieved with a large element of Pictish support. A claim to the Scottish throne through male descent was of course perfectly compatible with a similar claim to the Pictish throne through descent from the female royal line. However, in the absence of any Pictish genealogies, such a descent would be almost impossible to prove today. On the other hand, a hereditary claim to the Pictish throne would have been equally difficult to maintain in the ninth century, unless it was true. We can only look at the probabilities.

Kenneth (Cinioch, Ciniod, Kinat) is a name which occurs three times in the *Pictish Chronicle* before the accession of Kenneth mac Alpin,[9] but not at all in the early Scottish king lists. Alpin (Elpin) occurs twice among the Pictish kings, and the only appearance of this name among the Scottish kings, Alpin son of Echach (following Dungal son of Selbach), seems to be a mistake for Eochach son of Echach.[10] Kenneth's name and that of his father suggest a Pictish ancestry, and, if his paternal grandfather was a Dalriadan king, it is highly probable that his maternal grandfather was a Pictish king. The fact that the Picts accepted him as their ruler strongly suggests that he had as good a claim to the Pictish throne as he had to the Scottish one. Kenneth's brother, who succeeded him, was called

Donald (Domnall), a name as Scottish as Kenneth's name was Pictish; and his two sons, who followed Donald as kings, were called Constantine, after the great Pictish king who founded the first united kingdom of the Picts and Scots, and Aed, after the Dalriadan king who was Kenneth's great grandfather. It is perfectly possible that Constantine was Kenneth mac Alpin's maternal grandfather.

Kenneth mac Alpin was a Scot to the Scots and a Pict to the Picts. In a retrospective sense he had dual nationality, and was thus ideally suited to lead the new combined kingdom. It is quite possible that, having grown up during the reigns of Constantine and Oengus as a member of the Picto–Scottish royal family, he did not view himself exclusively as either a Pict or a Scot. Thus his rise to power represented neither a Scottish conquest of the Picts nor a Pictish conquest of the Scots, but rather the successful culmination of a bid for the throne of the joint Picto-Scottish kingdom. He was called King of the Picts (*rex Pictorum*) by contemporary annalists writing in Latin, probably because by far the larger part of his kingdom consisted of the old provinces of the Picts. But Latin was the language of the Church, not of the people, and he may well have been known to his own people, on both sides of the spine of Britain, as well as to the Irish across the sea, as King of Alba (*ri Albain*).

CHAPTER 15

Out of History into Mystery

The age of the Picts, as far as contemporary documentation goes, ended before the close of the ninth century. In the *Annals of Ulster*,[1] the last kings of the Picts whose deaths are recorded are Constantine son of Kenneth, in 876, and his brother Aed, in 878. Both are identified as *rex Pictorum*. However, if the age of the Picts came to an end, so too did the age of the Scots. The Scots of Dalriada were never referred to as 'Scots' by the Irish annalists, and their kings were recorded as kings of Dalriada (*rex Dalriatai, ri Dalriati*). The last king identified as a king of Dalriada in the annals is Donncorci, who died in 792. The Scots of Dalriada disappeared from the contemporary records nearly a hundred years before the Picts.

The disappearance of the Picts and the Scots from the contemporary records in the Irish annals is an illusion – there was no disappearance. We have only to look at the king lists to see that the succession of kings went on without a break. The one remarkable feature of these lists is that, from about the beginning of the ninth century, the Picts and the Scots were recognizing the same kings as their rightful rulers. Constantine son of Fergus, who became king of the Scots late on in his long reign over the Picts, was nonetheless accepted as having reigned over the Scots of Dalriada for 9 years, and was succeeded by his brother Oengus in both kingdoms. Perhaps the best analogy for Constantine's recognition as king by both the Picts and the Scots is James VI of Scotland, who became King of England in 1603, after reigning for 35 years in Scotland (though Constantine would certainly not have become king at the age of one, as James did!). Constantine's reign is in marked contrast to that of his predecessor, Oengus son of Fergus, who conquered Dalriada by military force in the previous century but was never recognized as king by the Scots.

These kings, in whom the separate dynasties of the Picts and the Scots were drawn into one, were known to the outside world first as kings of Fortren and later as kings of the Picts. From the beginning of the tenth century, when the Irish annalists began recording their obituaries in the vernacular, they are known as kings of Alba: the same dynasty, the same kingdom, the same people – just a change of language, from Latin to Gaelic, and a change of name. And, whatever we may choose to call that kingdom – Pictavia, Alba or Scotland – it continued to be subject to raids, attacks and indeed invasions by the Vikings, who soon established permanent colonies in Orkney and Caithness, in the Western Isles, and around Dublin, in Ireland. But to say that 'the Viking threat weakened Pictland and stimulated the Scots of Dalriada towards their eventual takeover of Pictland'[2] is simply not borne out by the contemporary records.

In 871 Olaf (Amlaiph) and Ivar (Imhar) came over from Dublin with two hundred ships and carried off a large number of prisoners, probably as slaves. In the *Annals of Ulster* these prisoners were recorded (in Latin) as being English, Britons and Picts.[3] It has been argued that, 'since the Scots were conspicuously absent from the list of slaves which the Norseman carried off from Scotland',[4] they were not subject to these attacks, and their king, Constantine, if not actually in alliance with the Norsemen, was at least happy to sit back and watch them softening up the Picts for him. But how can this be reconciled with the fact that Constantine was himself King of the Picts, as were his father, Kenneth mac Alpin, and his uncle, Donald mac Alpin, before him? The matter is clarified by the version of the Irish annals transcribed by MacFirbis, in which the same prisoners are stated (in the vernacular) to be Britons, Albans and Saxons.[5] The (Latin) Picts and the (Gaelic) Albans were the same people, and both names by this period were general terms covering the inhabitants of the combined Pictish and Dalriadan kingdoms. If there is any remaining doubt on this matter, it may be dispelled by reference to the *Annals of Inisfallen*, in which the following mixed Latin-Gaelic obituaries are to be found:[6]

820   *Mors Causantin meic Fergusa Rig Albain*
858   *Quies Cinaed macc Alpin Rig Albain*
862   *Mors Domnail meic Alpin Rig Albain*

The dynasty of Kenneth mac Alpin continued to rule over Alba, and when, in about 1070, the *Duan Albanach* was committed to writing, it was addressed to the learned men of Alban. But the author of the *Duan Albanach*, as it has come down to us, had a problem – a problem familiar to us in recent years as 'the problem of the Picts'. This problem, however, was not strictly his, so he disposed of it in three short verses before going on to hymn the praises of Fergus mac Erc and his descendants, who ruled over the Scots of Dalriada. These verses,[7] brief though they are, enable us to recognize the author's sources and how he used them.

> The Cruithne took it [Alba] afterwards,
> After coming from the plains of Erin,
> Seventy noble kings of them
> Possessed the Cruithnian plain.
>
> Cathluan was the first king of them,
> I tell unto you briefly,
> The last king of them was
> The brave hero Cusantin.

> The children of Eochadh after them
> Took Alban, after great wars,
> The children of Conaire, the mild man,
> The chosen of the strong Gael.

Seventy noble kings possessed the Cruithnian (Pictish) plain, that is to say the relatively low-lying country to the east of the mountainous spine of Britain. The number of kings suggests a familiarity with the king list contained in the *Pictish Chronicle*. And the fact that the last Pictish king was 'the brave hero Custantin' is a clear indication that the author had read some version of the Irish annals, in which Constantine son of Kenneth was the last king to be recorded as *rex Pictorum*. So far so good, but how was he to reconcile his own list of the (Scottish) kings of Alban with the former existence of such a long line of Pictish kings. The answer he came up with was simple and not at all unreasonable: war, 'great wars'. Who were these 'children of Eochadh' who took Alban after such great wars? In the next verse we find out that they were none other than Fergus son of Erc son of Eochadh and his brothers, Loarn and Aongus.

It is obvious to us now that there is a chronological inconsistency in this. Constantine, 'the last king of them' (the Picts), died in 876, and Comgall son of Domangart, grandson of Fergus, died in about 542. There is not the slightest possibility that 'the children of Eochadh' took Alban after the reign of Constantine, the last of the seventy Pictish kings. If, by 'the children of Eochadh', the author of the *Duan Albanach* meant 'the distant descendants of Eochadh', or if, by 'took Alban', he meant 'took the western part of Alban, west of the spine of Britain', we might have been able to accept his solution as reasonable. But whatever he meant, what he actually said was quite clear. For him, wars (even great wars) were short-lived in the historical timescale, and conquests were all or nothing. How did he manage to reach such a conclusion, when the sources that he had clearly consulted tell us quite a different story? There are two partial answers to this question. First, the Irish annals, when he consulted them, almost certainly had no AD dates in them. Second, there was very little reason to identify any of the kings in his (Alban) king list with any of those whose deaths were recorded by the Irish annalists, most of whom are mentioned by name only, with no suggestion that they were kings at all.

During the twelfth century, while the Irish annals continued to refer (in the vernacular) to the kings of Alba (Albania in contemporary Latin documents), there was an increasing tendency for Scottish writers to refer to their country as Scotia (the Latin equivalent of Scotland). It was a confusing situation. The author of the early twelfth-century *Metrical Prophecy* presented both names, with appropriate 'authority', and left his readers to judge for themselves: 'From Albanectus, great great grandson of Aeneas, it is called Albania: an ancient document proves it. From Scota, daughter of Pharaoh, king of Egypt, so the elders teach, Scotia has its name.'[8]

The introduction of this new name, for such it undoubtedly was,[9] did not pass without comment. One scholar, writing a description (in Latin) of Albania in 1165, said:

We gather in the histories and chronicles of the ancient Britons, and in the early records and annals of the Scots and Picts, that the country which is now wrongly called Scotia (*que nunc corrupte vocatur Scotia*) was long ago called Albania from Albanectus the younger son of Brutus the first king of the Britons of greater Britain.[10]

But in spite of such 'scholarly' objections, Scotland had come to stay, and its inhabitants, whether of Pictish (the great majority) or Dalriadan Scottish origin, would have been proud to call themselves Scots.

Geoffrey of Monmouth, in his *History of the Kings of Britain*, completed in about 1136, wrote that Albanectus, the youngest son of Brutus, 'took the region which is nowadays called Scotland in our language' and called it Albany after his own name.[11] Geoffrey, writing in Latin, allegedly from a Welsh original, referred to 'the Welsh tongue' in the previous sentence, and it seems that 'our language' must have been English. It is therefore worth looking at contemporary English language sources, among which the *Anglo-Saxon Chronicle* is the equivalent of the Irish annals. There are only occasional mentions of the Picts in the *Anglo-Saxon Chronicle*, and many of these are derived from Bede. The last of these is for the year 875, when the Picts were ravaged by the Danes, an event also recorded by the Irish annalists. The English, like the Welsh and Irish, referred to the united Picto–Scottish people in the ninth century as the Picts. But there is no mention at all of Alba or Albania.

The Picts disappeared from the *Anglo-Saxon Chronicle* before the end of the ninth century, but the Albans failed to materialize in their place. Instead we have the Scots and Scotland: Constantine king of the Scots in 926, Malcolm king of the Scots in 945, and the English king Athelstan ravaging Scotland in 933 or 934. These Scots were the same people as the Picts of the previous century: the same people, the same kingdom, the same dynasty, the same country . . . the same in all but name. In the Irish annals the change in name from Picts to Albans was not a real change at all, but simply reflected a change in the language in which the annals were written. In the *Anglo-Saxon Chronicle*, however, the language is English throughout. Why then did the Picts become Scots in these English records?

The *Anglo-Saxon Chronicle* up to the last quarter of the eighth century is a composite work brought together into one great national chronicle under the direction of Alfred the Great, King of Wessex from 871 to 899. From this time onwards the chronicle was continued, in the English language, as a record of contemporary events. We must therefore conclude that the English, or at least those whose culture emanated from Wessex, referred to the contemporary Picto–Scottish inhabitants of northern Britain as Scots and to their land as Scotland. Most of the earlier references to the Picts (*Peohtas*, etc) are probably translations from the Latin (some certainly from Bede's *Ecclesiastical History of the English People*). Once again, the disappearance of the Picts from contemporary sources seems to be an illusion created by the abandonment of Latin as the language of the annalists and chroniclers.

Throughout the tenth and eleventh centuries the Irish annalists continued to refer to the successors of Kenneth mac Alpin as kings of Alban, while the English chroniclers called them kings of the Scots. Then at last, from about the middle of the eleventh century, we hear the authentic voice of the kings themselves, encapsulated in the Latin texts of their few surviving charters.[12] Thus, in a charter of 1094 to Durham Cathedral, we read: 'I, Duncan, son of King Malcolm and manifest King of Scotland by inheritance, have given . . .'. A few decades earlier (1040–57) is a note in the register of the Priory of St Andrews, in which it is recorded that 'Macbeth, son of Finlach, and Gruoch, daughter of Bodhe, King and Queen of Scots, granted Kyrkenes to Almighty God and to the culdees of the island of Loch Leven'.

Half a century earlier than these charters is the 'Brechin Chronicle', introduced in the last chapter. This is written in Latin throughout, but the name of the country changed from Pictavia to Albania at about the beginning of the tenth century. After writing that Kenneth mac Alpin ruled Pictavia for 16 years, the late tenth-century compiler of the 'Brechin Chronicle' felt it necessary to explain that Pictavia was so called after the Picts. To him, and even more to his intended readers, Pictavia and the Picts were ancient history. But he continued to reproduce his source material, and we read, later in the reign of Kenneth mac Alpin (some time before 858), that the Danes wasted Pictavia as far as Cluny and Dunkeld. The last reference to Pictavia was in the reign of Donald son of Constantine (who died in 900). Then in the third year of Constantine son of Aed (902), the Norsemen ravaged Dunkeld and all of Albania. It is possible that in the source material for the 'Brechin Chronicle' there was a change in language from Latin to the vernacular at this date, as in the *Annals of Ulster*. When the Brechin compiler had occasion to refer to the people, he invariably called them Scots. By the time he was writing, the Picts were a barely remembered people of the distant past, and he and his fellow countrymen were Scots.

The people of Alba, who had been known to the Irish annalists (in Latin) as the Picts, were now, little over a hundred years later, calling themselves (also in Latin) Scots. It is sometimes doubted whether they had ever in fact called themselves Picts, though the description of Nechtan the great, in a document which must have originated in Abernethy, as 'king of all the provinces of the Picts' makes it almost certain that they did. We can, however, be fairly sure that they had not always called themselves Scots. Bede and Adomnan, both well-qualified witnesses, made it quite clear that in their time (late seventh and early eighth century) the Scots were restricted to the west of the mountainous spine of Britain. When and why did the Picts of central and eastern Scotland start calling themselves Scots? Before attempting to answer this question, it is worth looking at the situation through the eyes of an anonymous twelfth-century geographer,[13] particularly with regard to the region he called Arregaichel (variously spelt, and meaning the district of the Gaels).

Arregaichel, the modern Argyll, was described as being in the western part of Scotland, above the Irish Sea. It was also said, in a somewhat contradictory way, to be separated from Scotland by a range of mountains. It is in fact none other than the former kingdom of Dalriada, last mentioned in the *Annals of Ulster* in 989, when Gofraigh, son of Aralt, King of Inchegall, was slain in Dalriada. The first mention of Arregaichel in the same annals is in 1164. It is thought of as a sort of borderland between the Scots (*Scotti*) and the Irish (*Hibernenses*). The area is Scottish in the sense that it is an integral part of the Scottish kingdom, but at the same time it can be thought of as distinct from (the real) Scotland, because the people have so much more in common with the Irish. The anonymous author, writing in 1165, put forward several hypotheses to explain the general Irishness of the people of Arregaichel. Was it because the Irish were in the habit of landing there when they came on raiding expeditions to Britain? Did the Irish settle there after the Picts? Did the *Scotti Picti* (the Scoto-Pictish or Picto-Scottish people) settle here first, when they came over from Ireland? Or was it simply the result of the close proximity of Scotland and Ireland in this area?

From our point of view, the importance of this twelfth-century work lies not in the hypotheses presented, but in the very clear statement of the difference between the Irish-like people west of the mountains, in Arregaichel, and the Scottish people east of the mountains. The same distinction prevailed in the time of Bede and Adomnan, but then the Irish-like people west of the mountains were called *Scotti*, while their neighbours east of the mountains were called *Picti*. Once again, it is not the people who have changed, nor even in this instance the language, but just the name by which they are known. The Scots of Ireland became Irish (*Hibernenses*), because they lived in Ireland (*Hibernia*). That is sensible enough. And the Picts of northern Britain became Scots. This does not seem to be the result of a Scottish conquest, because the very people who are supposed to have conquered them, the Scots of Dalriada, themselves almost ceased to be Scots. So why did the Picts become Scots?

The Picts disappeared from the contemporary annals and chronicles simply because the Latin name (*Picti*) by which they had been known to the outside world for some six centuries went out of use. Meanwhile they were also gradually losing the one thing which, above all others, served to distinguish them from neighbouring peoples – their language. Precisely what that language was, or when it disappeared, we do not know. The earliest surviving Pictish manuscripts – the *Pictish Chronicle* and the ninth century St Luke's Gospel in the *Book of Deer* – were written in Latin, the international language of learning.

The Pictish language eventually gave way to the advancing tide of English from Northumbria. The northward march of the English language was probably the result of gradual diffusion, rather than any definable series of historical events. At any one time there was probably a bilingual zone between a Pictish-speaking area to the north and an English-speaking area to the south. If, over a period of time, a significant number of people north of this bilingual zone found it worth their while to learn English, while at the same time other people towards the southern edge of the area gave up speaking Pictish, the bilingual zone would gradually have migrated northwards through the Pictish-speaking country. On this model, as the Pictish-speaking area got smaller there would have been less and less incentive for any outsider to learn the language and its fate would be sealed.

Over the centuries the English language enjoyed much greater success than the English armies. In 1066 the English were defeated by the Normans at Hastings. Within a few years the whole country was under Norman rule, but the English language survived. In 1314 the English were defeated by the Scots at

Bannockburn, the decisive battle in the Scottish war of independence. When, in 1375, John Barbour, Archdeacon of Aberdeen, wrote his epic poem *Brus*, celebrating the events of this war, he wrote it in the language of the people – English! The English failed to conquer the Scots, just as surely as the Romans before them had failed to conquer the Picts. But when, in eleventh-century documents, the kings are first described as *Rex Scotiae* or *Rex Scottorum*, these titles probably represent Latin translations of English language usage current at the time. St Andrews, where the earliest of these documents originated, is likely to have been one of the first cities north of the Forth to adopt the English language. The Picts began to call themselves Scots as and when they adopted the English language, though why the English called them Scots in the first place we can only guess.

The Picts had finally lost their identity. Their language had succumbed to the inexorable advance of English and, probably as a direct result of this, they were now using their English language label and calling themselves Scots. The Picts had survived unconquered, but they had survived almost without a trace. By the twelfth century, had it not been for the documentary evidence discussed in previous chapters, the Picts might as well never have existed. They would have been a forgotten people, neither more nor less significant than any other unnamed tribe of the late prehistoric Iron Age. But there was documentary evidence and the Picts were not prehistoric. And yet the land where they had once ruled supreme was now in the hands of the Scots. What had happened to the Picts? The problem of the Picts was ready and waiting for the first unwary historian who might try to solve it, and it had not long to wait.

CHAPTER 16

Medieval Historians and the Problem of the Picts

By the time the first attempts to interpret the history of Scotland were being made, in the eleventh century, the separate identity of the Pictish and Scottish kingdoms had receded so far into the past that the essential unity of the kingdom, whether it was called Alba or Scotland, was taken for granted. It followed from this assumption that, since there were independent lists of Pictish and Scottish kings, these kingdoms must have succeeded one another rather than coexisted side by side. Thus in the *Duan Albanach* (1057–93), which was mainly concerned with the Scottish kings, the Picts (*Cruithnigh*) were there first and were overthrown by Fergus mac Erc and his brothers 'after great wars'.[1] The last King of the Picts was recorded as 'the brave hero Cusantin', a statement likely to be derived from the Irish annals where he is called *Constantin mac Cinaeda rex Pictorum*, and he died in 876.[2] Actually, his brother Aedh, who died 2 years later, is also called *rex Pictorum* rather than *ri Albain*, so poetic licence may have had something to do with the choice.

The first Scottish historian to consider this problem seems to have been commissioned to draw up a pedigree for King William, known to his contemporaries as William Rufus but better known to us as William the Lion. His *Cronica regum Scottorum*,[3] written in 1165, begins with a list of kings and the lengths of their reigns. This agrees with the *Duan Albanach* in making Fergus mac Erc the first of the line of Chonare to hold the kingdom of Alba, but defines Alba as reaching from the spine of Britain (*a monte Drumalban*) to the Irish Sea (broadly equivalent to the old kingdom of Dalriada or the modern county of Argyll). Kenneth mac Alpin was given a special place in the list as the first king of the Scots (*Kynedus filius Alpini primus rex Scottorum*). There is no evidence that Kenneth was ever called King of the Scots by his contemporaries. He was *rex Pictorum* in Latin and almost certainly *ri Albain* in Gaelic. But the statement that he was the first king of the Scots does emphasize his importance as the founder of the dynasty which had ruled over the combined Picto–Scottish kingdom for over three hundred years. It is equivalent to the statement made in the *Synchronisms of Flann Mainistreach* (1014–22) that 'he was the first king, who possessed the kingdom of Scone, of the Gael'.[4]

When it came to the pedigree itself, the very king who was celebrated as the founder of the dynasty provided the greatest problem. In common with almost all the kings in the *Pictish Chronicle* the identity of his paternal grandfather is a complete mystery. But the author of this manuscript was either quite unaware of the Pictish king lists, or had the good sense to disregard them: he was, after all, concerned with the pedigree of a Scottish king. The Scottish king lists, on the other hand, provided much more promising material. But for this particular genealogist there was a problem. There was only one Alpin in the list, and he was far too early. There were only two options open to him. He had either to invent a suitable Alpin, or make use of the one that was already there and cheat a little. He chose the latter course and placed Kenneth mac Alpin immediately after Alpin son of Eochaid the Venomous (*Alpin filius Eochal venenosi*) in his list, thus missing out eleven intervening kings recorded by Flann Mainistreach and telescoping about a hundred years of history: a small price to pay for a royal genealogy reaching back, through Fergus mac Erc and Jafeth, son of Noah, to Adam, son of the living God.

The first Scottish historian to take account of the Pictish as well as the Scottish kings, set them out in one long list entitled *Cronica brevis*.[5] He divided his list into three parts:

1   the Scots, who reigned before the Picts for a total of 260 years and 3 months;
2   the Picts, totalling 1061 years;
3   the Scots, who came after the Picts, totalling 337 years and 5 months to the time of writing (1187).

By adding these totals together, he found that the kingdom of Scotland (*Scotia*) had been founded in 448 BC (the minor errors in his arithmetic do not seriously affect the issue).

The lists begin with Fergus mac Erc, who was the first to reign in Scotland beyond the spine of Britain. The Scottish kings are then listed, with their reign lengths, as far as Alpin son of Eochaid the Venomous (*Aropin filius Hethed annune*). This is followed by the complete list of Pictish kings up to Drust son of Ferat, the immediate predecessor of Kenneth mac Alpin. The last section of the list traces the well-known dynasty of Scottish kings from Kenneth mac Alpin. The Pictish list is the first of the group B copies of the *Pictish Chronicle*, and the early Scottish section is very similar to that in the *Cronica regum Scottorum*. Placing the Pictish kings, as it were, in a sandwich between the earlier and later Scottish kings gave the impression that the Picts were to be viewed as interlopers in a kingdom which should have been Scottish right from the start. There is of course no more historical truth in this sequence than in the alternative view, given in the *Duan Albanach*, that all of the Pictish kings up to Constantine reigned before the arrival of Fergus mac Erc and his brothers. One rather curious result of this sequence, which may not have occurred to its author, is that it makes a complete nonsense of the genealogy of the later Scottish kings. In the *Cronica regum Scottorum* a hundred years of history was telescoped so that Kenneth mac Alpin could be linked to his supposed father. In the *Cronica brevis* this same supposed father and son are separated by over a thousand years of Pictish rule.

The arrangement of these lists should be viewed as an interpretation of very limited source material (probably little more than the king lists themselves) on the basis of an entirely false assumption that, throughout the period under consideration, there had been only one kingdom in Scotland. Bearing this in mind, it is interesting to see how the three separate sections of the list were joined together.

The first list ends with Alpin son of Eochaid, who 'reigned for three years and was killed in Galloway after he had completely destroyed it and laid it waste, and then the kingdom of the Scots was transferred into the kingdom of the Picts' (*tunc translatum est regnum Scottorum in regnum Pictorum*). Just exactly what is meant by this transference is not clear. There is no suggestion of invasion by a conquering Pictish army, which would be the usual explanation for a change of government. Instead it seems more like a subtle metamorphosis after the untimely death of the heroic Scottish king. The sympathy of the reader is thus directed towards the Scots, and the story is rendered politically correct.

The last king in the Pictish section of the list, Drust son of Ferat, reigned for 3 years and 'was killed at Forteviot, or according to others at Scone, by the Scots'. He is followed immediately by Kenneth mac Alpin, who

> reigned for sixteen years over the Scots, after the Picts had been destroyed , and died in Forteviot and was buried on Iona, where the three sons of Erc, namely Fergus, Loarn and Tenagus were buried. He led the Scots with wonderful cunning from Argyll into the land of the Picts (*Hic mira caliditate duxit Scotos de Ergadia in terram Pictorum*).

The 1251 version of the combined Pictish and Scottish king lists[6] gives the same sequence as the *Cronica brevis*, and the changes of regime are explained in virtually identical wording. The next edition,[7] together with other material on the origin of the Picts and the Scots, was written at a time of national crisis, following the unfortunate death of Alexander III in 1286, 'from which arose great evil'. Alone among the documents printed by Skene, this one is in Norman French, translated into that language presumably to satisfy the interest of some Anglo–Norman nobleman, perhaps even one of the claimants to the Scottish throne, such as John Balliol or Robert Bruce the elder. It begins with an exasperated statement of the now familiar problem that

> according to the Chronicles of Scotland, there never was such difficulty as that which would set down in writing their kings of the direct line, who entirely failed in the time of three kings successively, each the son of the other.

The last phrase is more difficult to understand than the lists themselves, since it seems to imply that there was only one failure after the last of the three kings. The lists are ordered in the same way as before: early Scots, Picts and later Scots.

The list of the early Scottish kings is prefaced by an account of Gaidelus and his wife Scota, the daughter of Pharaoh King of Egypt, and how their descendants settled first in Ireland and then, under Fergus mac Erc (*Fergus fitz*

Ferthair de Ireland), in the west of Scotland. He was the first to call himself King of Scotland (*roy Descoce*). The death of Alpin son of Eochaid the Venomous is described in greater detail than in the earlier Latin versions of the list, though the extra material is probably no more than literary embellishment of the otherwise bare 'facts'.

> He was killed in Galloway, after he had destroyed it, by a single man who lay in wait for him in a thick wood overhanging the entrance of the ford of a river, as he rode among his people. He was the last of the Scots, who at that time reigned immediately before the Picts.

The Pictish section of the list is preceded by an account of how the Picts set sail from Scythia and landed in northern Britain in the time of Vespasian and a British king called Marius son of Arviragon. After many battles the Pictish leader, Roderic, was slain near Carlisle, and Marius (with quite uncalled for generosity) allowed the Picts to settle in the far north. This is followed by the old story of the Picts having no women and eventually getting wives from Ireland. The source of this story, as set down in the account, is to be found in Geoffrey of Monmouth's *Historia regum Brittaniae*.[8] The Pictish list ends with Drust son of Ferat (*Drust fitz Feradhach*), who was 'the last king of the Picts, and was killed at Scone by treason'. The second list of Scottish kings is introduced in the person of Redda, recorded elsewhere as the eponymous ancestor of the Scots of Dalriada.

> As the chronicles testify, a son of a king of Ireland called Redda, arrived in Galloway, and, partly by prowess and by affinity of Irish blood, with whom the Picts were mixed, occupied that country, and also Argyll and others of the isles, the issue of whom, who called themselves Scoty, always plotted against the Picts until in the time of this Drust, son of Feradhach, the Scots contrived a conspiracy, and at a general council were privately armed, and in the council house slew the aforesaid king and all the great lords of the Picts, who did not think of evil. They sent afterwards for such others as they wished, and slew them as they came, so that they did as they desired; and from that time henceforth the kingdom of the Picts failed, which had lasted for eleven hundred and eighty seven years, and the kingdom of the Scots recommenced, which had commenced before the Picts, four hundred and forty three years before the incarnation. The Picts destroyed in this manner, Kynet son of Alpin reigned over the Scots, and was the first king of the Scots after the Picts.

The fullest, and also the earliest, version of this story was written by Giraldus Cambrensis in his *De Instructione Principium* (1214). The Latin text was printed by Skene and a translation by A.O. Anderson.[9]

> After the island had been occupied by the Saxons, as we have said, and peace had been established with the Picts, the Scots, who were allied to the Picts and had been invited by them to the land, seeing that although fewer in number, because of the nearness of Ireland, the Picts were yet far superior in arms and

valour, they betook themselves to their customary and as it were innate treacheries, in which they excel other nations. They brought together as to a banquet all the nobles of the Picts, and taking advantage of their perhaps excessive potation and the gluttony of both drink and food, they noted their opportunity and drew out the bolts which held up the boards; and [the Picts] fell into the hollows of the benches on which they were sitting, [caught] in a strange trap up to their knees, so that they could never get up; and [the Scots] immediately slaughtered them all, tumbled together everywhere and taken suddenly and unexpectedly, and fearing nothing of the sort from allies and confederates, men bound to them by benefits and companions in their wars. And thus the more warlike and powerful nation of the two peoples wholly disappeared; and the other, by far inferior in every way, as a reward obtained in the time of so great treachery, have held to this day the whole land from sea to sea, and called it Scotland after their name.

Even in translation, the finer details of this story are somewhat obscure, but its general tone could hardly be clearer. The sympathies of the reader are directed towards the Picts, whose greatest sin seems to have been their somewhat excessive enjoyment of a good party. The Scots, on the other hand, are shown in a very bad light, with references to their innate treachery and their general inferiority to the Picts. This story cannot be the work of a Scottish historian, who would have been much more likely to record great battles and famous victories to explain the disappearance of the Picts. There are two possible sources. It could be a genuine Pictish tradition, preserved somewhere in Scotland by people who had managed to retain a sense of Pictish identity (if indeed they had ever thought of themselves as Picts) through centuries of being Scots. Alternatively, it could have been derived from some external literary source. Two such sources would have been well known to Giraldus. Geoffrey of Monmouth, writing nearly a hundred years earlier, had used a similar story[10] to explain the failure of the Britons to stem the tide of the Saxon advance, and an earlier version of the same story was recorded by Nennius,[11] early in the ninth century. These traditions survived because a remnant of the British people remained unconquered in the highlands of Wales and the south-west, and their national identity, culture and language were preserved intact. It has been suggested recently that these stories were themselves derived from a much earlier folk memory, originating in the prehistoric Bronze Age.[12]

A remarkable feature of this story, as told by Giraldus, is the total lack of names. He did not attribute the massacre of the Pictish nobility to Kenneth mac Alpin. Indeed, having written two books on Ireland, he may well have been familiar with the Irish annals and with Kenneth mac Alpin as a king of the Picts. His problem was our problem. What had happened to the great Pictish nation, which had been so powerful almost to the end of the ninth century, and whose place in his own time and for centuries before had been taken by the Scots. The contemporary records were silent on the matter, and yet there must have been a reason for the disappearance of a complete nation. It seems likely that the massacre at the banquet was a modification of the familiar British story, used to explain an apparently similar situation. In fact, as we have seen, the similarity was more apparent than real. The disappearance of the Picts was an illusion created by linguistic changes.

The next edition of the combined Pictish and Scottish king lists,[13] after recording the death of Alexander III, bewailed the state of the country, which 'has been silent, without a king, for as many years as have intervened'. It must therefore have been written some time before the general recognition of Robert Bruce as king, and certainly before his great victory over the English at Bannockburn in 1314. In this list the order of the sections is changed so that the Picts come first and are followed by the early and then the later Scottish kings. The anonymous author of the list was familiar with Bede's *Ecclesiastical History of the English People*, in which he recognized the one event which could also be identified in the Pictish king list, namely the conversion of Brude son of Maelcon by St Columba. At this point he inserted a selection of important dates, culled from Bede's work (some with scribal errors, indicated below). The dates are as follows:

Arrival of St Columba among the Picts, 565 (as given by Bede)
Death of St Columba, 582 (should be 597, 32 years after his arrival: xxxii, not xvii)
Arrival of the English in Britain, 469 (cccclxix in error, ccccxlix in Bede)
Battle of Mount Badon, 44 years later (as given by Bede)
Battle of Dexastan, in which Aidan mac Gabran was defeated by Ethelfrid (Cadfred), 513 (dxiii in error, dciii in Bede)

Unfortunately, owing to differences in spelling, he was unable to identify Bede's Aidan son of Gabran with the Edhan son of Goueran in the early Scottish king list, which in any case does not mention that king's defeat at Dexastan. Had he been able to make that identification, he might have realized that the Pictish kings and the earlier Scottish kings were in part contemporary.

There is no mention of the massacre at the banquet here. The explanation of the end of the early Scottish kings and the beginning of the later ones is very close to that of the earlier Latin editions, quite regardless of the fact that an explanation is no longer required. The Picts have been removed from the middle of the 'sandwich' and Kenneth mac Alpin (the first of the later kings) is once again allowed to follow immediately after his supposed father, Alpin son of Eochaid the Venomous (the last of the earlier kings). We are told of the death of Alpin in Galloway and then that the kingdom of the Scots was transferred to the land of the Picts (*ad terram Pictorum* instead of *ad regnum Pictorum*, as in earlier editions). The sum of the years from the time of Fergus mac Erc to the time of Alpin was then given as 307 years and 3 months, though the actual total of the individual reign lengths is 285 years and 3 months. Kenneth mac Alpin was then introduced, exactly as in the earlier versions, as having reigned for 16 years after the destruction of the Picts (*destructis Pictis*), died in Forteviot and been buried in Iona alongside the three sons of Erc. The destruction of the Picts in this edition seems rather unnecessary, as they were supposed to have disappeared some three hundred years earlier – but the words were there, and the words were copied.

So what can we learn from the work of these medieval historians? The answer depends on which period we are interested in. If we are concerned with the later period, after the union of the kingdoms under Kenneth mac Alpin, the king lists are supplemented with a fair selection of contemporary historical events. For the earlier periods, however, the lists are bare. And this was not for want of effort on the part of the historians. They extracted information from the sources available to them, but these sources were woefully inadequate. From the lives of saints and other church records, they were able to note (sometimes incorrectly) the foundation of churches by various Pictish kings. From the life of St Adomnan it was noted that Brude son of Bile was his contemporary. But that was all, and it did not amount to much in the way of historical knowledge. It is fairly clear that they did not have access to the Irish annals, and even Bede, when at last he was discovered, was not much help.

One thing is abundantly clear from the lists discussed above: the period before the accession of Kenneth mac Alpin was a complete mystery to the medieval historians of Scotland. As the author of the Norman French edition wrote in his introduction, 'there never was such difficulty as that which would set down in writing their kings of the direct line'. Their conclusions were mostly wrong, and that for two reasons. First, they had a preconceived idea that all of the kings in the lists, whether Pictish or Scottish, should follow one another in a single long succession. Second, the source material available to them was totally inadequate for the task they had set themselves.

It is quite evident to us now that most of their understanding of this remote period was quite wrong, and few modern historians would take their conclusions seriously. Yet, in spite of this, their oft repeated statements – that Kenneth mac Alpin was the first of the Scots to reign after the Picts, or that he led the Scots out of Argyll into the land of the Picts, or that his reign followed the destruction of the Picts – are widely accepted as records of genuine tradition. No wonder we still have problems with this period of history. If we consider the contrary evidence of the contemporary sources, these statements are much more easily interpreted as part of the medieval historical interpretation, which was necessary to explain the supposed change from Pictish to Scottish rule. In fact, it is much more likely that the only thing that was, in the long run, destroyed was the Pictish language and the name by which the Pictish people were known in contemporary Latin texts, and neither of these can be attributed to Kenneth mac Alpin.

CHAPTER 17

Pictish Symbols: Hieroglyphics or Heraldry?

The Pictish symbol stones are, of all things Pictish, the most tantalizing. It is universally agreed that they are Pictish and that the symbols must have conveyed a perfectly clear meaning at the time; and yet that meaning remains as obscure today as that of the Egyptian hieroglyphics before the discovery of the Rosetta stone. How can we set about the task of interpreting them?

Anthony Jackson, in his book on the symbol stones,[1] made use of a comparison between the Picts and the Na-khi, a remote highland tribe near the border between China and Tibet. Ethnographic models have been widely used in archeological interpretation, and have been particularly successful in the study of prehistoric societies and how they might have functioned. For more specific studies, such as the interpretation of Pictish symbols, the distance, both in space and time, between the Picts and the Na-khi would seem to present an almost insuperable barrier. It need come as no surprise therefore that, while Jackson produced a theory for the political and social background to the production of the symbol stones, he failed to produce a transcription or a translation for a single symbol. Egyptian hieroglyphics can be read and translated. Pictish symbols cannot.

Pictish symbols most commonly occur in pairs, and only rarely in groups of more than four. It is fairly clear, therefore, that each symbol must represent a whole word or concept rather than an individual letter or syllable. In an attempt to interpret these symbols, it might be useful to make a comparison with the inscribed stones of the same general period in Wales. Thanks to a rather closer contact with the Roman occupation of Britain, these stones are inscribed in Latin and can be read and translated. The practice of setting up standing stones is widespread, both in Wales and in Scotland, and has its roots in the depths of prehistory. There seems no good reason why the inscribed stones of Wales and the symbol stones of Scotland should not both be viewed as a continuation of that practice into the historic period. If we take this as a starting point, then the inscriptions on the Welsh stones may provide a guide to the interpretation of the symbols on the Scottish ones.

The majority of the Welsh inscriptions[2] fall into one or other of four simple forms:

1   'Name';
2   'Name', son or daughter (occasionally wife) of 'Name';
3   Here lies 'Name';
4   Here lies 'Name', son or daughter (or wife) of 'Name'.

Sometimes additional information was added to inscriptions of this basic pattern: the occupation of the deceased (priest, bishop, doctor), the tribe (Ordovician, Elmetian) to which he belonged or the name of the person who erected the stone. Sometimes the inscriptions record the death or burial of several members of the same family. There has been much discussion about whether or not the Pictish symbol stones are gravestones. In the present discussion, no preconceived opinion was formed, though the circumstances of recent finds strongly suggest that this is the case[3]. It just so happens that the majority of the contemporary Welsh monuments can be identified, by their inscriptions, as either gravestones or memorials to the dead.

From an analysis of nearly 170 Welsh inscribed stones, it can be shown that by far the commonest words or elements in the inscriptions are names. After names, the next most common element is 'son of' or 'daughter of', which occurs in over forty per cent of the inscriptions. After this, 'here lies' is found on a little over thirty per cent. Do these simple statistics provide any clues to the interpretation of the Pictish symbols?

Pictish symbol stones are of two broad types, long known as Class I and Class II. The symbols on the Class I stones are incised, whereas those on the Class II stones are carved in relief. A further distinction between the two classes is that on the Class I stones there is no additional ornament, while the symbols on the Class II stones often seem subordinate to a mass of other pictorial material. The Class II stones are also generally carved on both faces, with the symbols on one side and a massive Christian cross, with interlace design, on the other. An interpretation of the Pictish symbols, if it is to have any chance of success, should begin with the Class I stones, on which the basic message is uncontaminated by extraneous material. It should also be noted that many of the symbol stones are fragmentary and may therefore display incomplete 'texts'. The sample for initial study will consist of Class I stones which are complete and on which the symbols are clearly legible. This group contains sixty-six stones and will be analysed below.

Some fifty different Pictish symbols have been recognized. These include: animals' heads, birds (eagle, goose), other animals (fish, serpent, boar, bull, dog), the 'Pictish beast' (often referred to as an elephant, but more probably a stylized dolphin), and a variety of inorganic designs (double disc and Z-rod, crescent and V-rod, tuning fork, and mirror and comb). Not all are universally recognized as 'symbols', that is to say designs with a meaning beyond their artistic or ornamental value. Among all of these, the mirror and comb symbol is generally agreed to have a different function from all the others. It is almost always found immediately below a pair of other symbols and, it has been suggested, 'tells us about the relationship between the other two symbols above it'[4]. The comb is sometimes missing from this symbol. The symbols in the selected sample of Class I stones occur in the following arrangements:

One symbol	4
Two symbols	36
Three symbols	1
Four symbols	1
One symbol, mirror, comb	1
Two symbols, mirror, comb	14
Two symbols, mirror	9

The dominance of the two-symbol arrangement is clearly demonstrated in this sample and amounts to almost ninety per cent of the total. The mirror and comb symbol (or the mirror by itself) is found on thirty-six per cent of the sample. If the Welsh inscriptions are to be used as a guide, most of the symbols should represent the names of individuals, while the mirror (with or without the comb) might represent either 'son (or daughter) of' or 'here lies'. Let us now consider these possibilities in turn.

The possible use of the double disc and Z-rod symbol to represent the name Drust (Drest, Drosten) has already been discussed in Chapter 10. It is carved on a rock at the entrance to Trusty's Hill, a coastal hillfort near Gatehouse of Fleet; on the Drosten stone, in the collection at St Vigean's, near Arbroath; and on several silver objects which may be connected with the long reign of Drust son of Erp in the fifth century. To anyone who has made a study of the Pictish symbol stones, one of their most striking features must be the extraordinary abundance of a few symbols (the crescent and V-rod, and the double disc and Z-rod in particular) and the relative scarcity of many others. In the lists published by Jackson[5] there are 425 legible symbols: 82 crescent and V-rod (19 per cent); 61 double disc and Z-rod (14 per cent); 48 Pictish 'elephant' (11 per cent); 20 fish (5 per cent); and so on. What about Pictish names?

The *Pictish Chronicle* provides a sample of Pictish names, which can be supplemented from the Irish annals. For the period from Drust son of Erp, in the fifth century, to the last Pictish kings before Kenneth mac Alpin, we can assemble a sample of 90 names, among which Drust is the commonest with 13 occurrences (14½ per cent); followed by Brude (Bridei) with 8 occurrences (9 per cent); Talorgan with 7 occurrences (8 per cent); and then Nechtan, Garthnach, Elpin, Ciniod (Cinaed) and Oengus (Onnist) with 4 occurrences each. The frequency distributions of names and symbols can be represented in the form of bar diagrams and are sufficiently similar to be consistent with the hypothesis that the symbols represent names. Assuming for the moment that this is the correct interpretation, we must now turn our attention to the special case of the mirror and comb symbol.

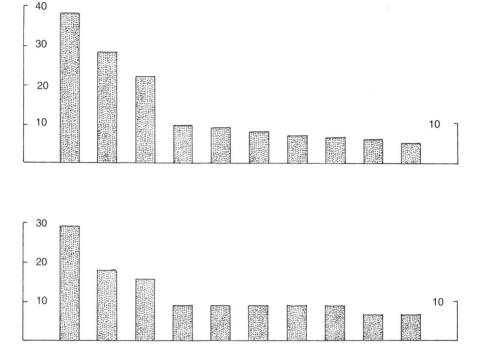

Bar diagrams comparing the relative abundance of the ten most common Pictish symbols (above) with the ten most common Pictish names (below).

The mirror might be considered an appropriate symbol for a son or daughter, representing, as it were, the concept of the child being the image of the parent. Attractive though this possibility is, however, it gives rise to a problem with the most common of all symbol arrangements, namely two symbols by themselves, without the mirror and comb. If it was argued that a son-to-father relationship was to be understood between the symbols of such pairs, then the addition of the mirror (and comb) to represent just such a relationship on other stones would seem superfluous. If two individuals are named in the Welsh inscriptions, the relationship between them is invariably stated. It seems likely then that some relationship between the two symbols of a pair was to be understood and that the mirror and comb must represent something quite different, such as 'here lies'. It might represent peace at last, after the struggles of life on earth, when there was often too little time to look in the mirror and comb one's hair. It might represent a view of the afterlife as some sort of reflection of the familiar life on earth. Who knows? Whatever the exact meaning, this type of interpretation leaves the mirror, with or without its accompanying comb, as an optional extra on a well-designed tombstone.

Any further progress in reading the Pictish symbols, if they represent personal names, must depend either on connecting individual stones with events in the all

Left: Class I symbol stone at Strathmiglo (Fife), found in 1969 and set up near the entrance to the cemetery: it is a basic two-symbol design on a rough stone pillar. Tuning fork symbol (for Nechtan) over (son of) deer's head (unidentified name). Right: Class I symbol stone (replica) at Dunnichen (Angus): two symbols plus mirror and comb. Stylized plant (?) symbol (unidentified name) over (son of) double disc and Z-rod (for Drust or Drosten), with mirror and comb (symbols for 'Rest in peace' or 'Here lies'). This is an individual memorial; nothing to do with the famous battle of Nechtansmere, fought nearby in AD 685.

too limited historical record, or on somehow decoding the symbols and matching them to names with appropriate meanings. The double disc and Z-rod, for example, might be interpreted as the clashing of cymbals, representing thunder, crossed by forked lightning. The name Tristan (Drosten in Pictish), probably represented by this symbol, may be related to the Welsh word *trystau*, meaning thunder. First of all, however, it is worth returning to the Drosten stone, on which the symbols may be interpreted by reference to an inscription on the same stone.

The Drosten stone has a cross flanked by intricately interwoven animals on one face and, on the other, a medley of wild animals with a huntsman armed with a crossbow in the bottom left-hand corner. The symbols, a double disc and Z-rod above a simple crescent (without V-rod), with a mirror and comb close by, are placed in the midst of the animals, rather than being given pride of place at the top of the stone. The general impression conveyed by this stone is that, while it is clearly a Christian memorial, the image of heaven is that of 'the happy hunting

Reverse of Hilton of Cadboll cross slab: relief design in two square panels surrounded by ornamental border. Above the top panel is a double disc and Z-rod symbol (for Drust or Drosten). In the upper panel are two symbols: the crescent and V-rod (for Brude) over (son of) two discs (unidentified name). The top symbol is clearly separated from the other two, contained within the panel, and may perhaps represent the man who had the stone carved and set up. The lower panel contains a hunting scene, two robed figures blowing trumpets, and the mirror and comb symbols, all of which in their different ways seem to be symbolic of death (Photo: National Museums of Scotland).

ground'. This theme is also represented on the Hilton of Cadboll stone (now in the National Museum in Edinburgh) in a well-defined square panel, with the mirror and comb symbols (clearly nothing to do with the hunt) in the top left-hand corner. The association makes sense if the mirror and comb symbols and the hunting scene both refer in their different ways to the afterlife. In the hunting panel on the Hilton of Cadboll stone, and also on the roadside cross slab at Aberlemno, there are two robed figures in the top right-hand corner blowing trumpets. Their robes are not only highly unsuitable for the hunt but also quite unlike the square-cut coats and tunics generally worn by the Picts. It is possible that these trumpeters are angels (though without the usual wings) come to summon the dead: yet another symbolic reference to death, this time a Christian one. Adomnan, in his *Life of St Columba*, makes numerous references to the appearance of angels to conduct the souls of the departed to heaven, but as he does not describe them, apart from their brightness, and makes no mention of either wings or trumpets, it is difficult to be certain of the identity of these particular figures.

Down near the bottom of one side of the Droston stone, in a clearly outlined square panel, is the inscription. This is generally transcribed as *Drosten ipe Uoret ett Forcus*, with *ipe* presumably being a Pictish word for 'son of', and *ett* representing the Latin word for 'and'. This reading gives three names, whereas there are only two symbols (excluding the mirror and comb).

The inscription on the Droston stone occupies only about half of the panel in

Class I symbol stone at Aberlemno (Angus): two symbols plus mirror and comb. Serpent (unidentified name) over (son of) double disc and Z-rod (for Drust or Drosten), with mirror and comb (symbols for 'Rest in Peace' or 'Here Lies').

which it is set. Either it was never completed, which seems unlikely in view of the fine quality of the ornamental work on the rest of the stone, or (a possibility not generally considered) it was subsequently defaced and the lower part of the inscription intentionally erased. The top two lines reach right across the panel, whereas the third is shorter by two letters and the fourth by five, after which there is room for three more lines. The inscription might therefore have read *Drosten ipe Uoret ett For . . . Cus . . .*. There may only have been two names on the inscription, Drosten and Uoret, and the addition of Forcus as a name looks unlikely, in view of the letters missing after *For*. The crescent therefore seems to be the symbol for the name Uoret.

Names beginning with U or W, such as Urguist (Uurguist, Wirguist), Uredeg (Wredech), Wroid and Wrad, which are found in the group A versions of the *Pictish Chronicle*, become Fergus, Ferath (Feradhegh), Frud (Feret) and Ferat of the group B versions of the chronicle. The Uoret of the inscription would thus become Foret. Indeed it is quite possible that the Drosten son of Uoret commemorated in this unique inscription is Drust son of Ferat, the last of the independent Pictish kings to succumb to the unification of the kingdoms under Kenneth mac Alpin. If this interpretation is correct, then the Drosten stone is indeed a historic monument, and the complete inscription may have contained material considered politically unsuitable by the new regime.

Left: Class II cross slab by roadside at Aberlemno (Angus); right: relief design in four panels on reverse. Pictish symbols in top panel: crescent and V-rod (for Brude) over (son of) double disc and Z-rod (for Drust or Drosten). Hunting scene in middle panel (possibly representing the afterlife as the 'happy hunting ground') with two robed figures with trumpets (possibly angels come to summon the dead). Centaur in bottom left panel, and David in bottom right panel, with sheep and harp.

The *Pictish Chronicle*, as a written record, probably had its origin in the church at Abernethy and, among the very few pieces of historical detail it contains, is a record of the founding of that church by Nechtan the Great, king of all the provinces of the Picts. The oldest surviving building at Abernethy is the great, red sandstone, round tower, dating from the eleventh century. Much earlier than this, however, is a fragment of a Class I symbol stone, which was recovered from the foundations of a house nearby and set up at the foot of the tower. This stone displays two symbols, the tuning fork above a crescent and V-rod. Either side of the tuning fork are a hammer and anvil, which, like the mirror and comb, are outside the normal run of Pictish symbols and may be interpreted as meaning some sort of manufacture. This fragment is probably all that remains of a symbol stone recording the construction of the original timber church at Abernethy, towards the end of the fifth century. If this is so, the tuning fork may be the symbol for Nechtan. The lower of the two symbols, the crescent and V-rod, is the most abundant of all the Pictish symbols and its interpretation is therefore correspondingly important.

On the Abernethy symbol stone, the crescent and V-rod may represent the

Mutilated Class I symbol stone at Abernethy (Fife): tuning fork symbol (for Nechtan), flanked by hammer and anvil (representing manufacture in general and, in this instance, built this church) over crescent and V-rod (for St Bride or Brigid).

name of Nechtan's father, though, if the stone is correctly interpreted as a foundation stone rather than a tombstone, this is not necessarily the most obvious reading. Nechtan, according to the *Pictish Chronicle*, was the son of Erip or Wirp, a name not found anywhere else in the Pictish records and therefore unlikely to be represented by such an abundant and widespread symbol as the crescent and V-rod. If not Nechtan's father, the lower symbol may represent the name of some official associated with him at Abernethy – perhaps his architect – or maybe the local tribal chief, under whose supervision the work might have been carried out.

Unfortunately we have no means of knowing the names of such people, or even if they ever existed. There is, however, another possibility, and this is that the stone records essentially the same information as is preserved in the *Pictish Chronicle*, namely that Nechtan dedicated the church to St Brigid. St Brigid, also known as St Bride, bore a name which was barely distinguishable from the Pictish name Brude (Bridei, Bruide) and might conveniently have been represented by the same symbol. It is therefore quite likely that the crescent and V-rod is the symbol for Brude, a possibility consistent with the importance of Brude as a Pictish name.

Another stone with possible historical connections is the cross slab in Aberlemno churchyard. This is a Class II stone with a splendid battle scene which should be read like a strip cartoon, finishing in the bottom right-hand corner, with the defeated enemy, unhorsed, and a scavenging raven wasting no

Left: cross slab in Aberlemno churchyard; right: reverse showing battle between two Pictish armies, the victors on the left and the vanquished on the right. The leaders of the two armies are represented by the symbols above. Which was the battle? Who were the leaders?

time to exploit the carnage. The winning army is shown on the left and the defeated army on the right. Above the battle scene are two symbols: the notched rectangle and Z-rod, very prominent and almost central, and the 'triple disc', tucked in to the right at a slightly lower level. It looks as if these symbols refer respectively to the victor and vanquished. If the battle could be identified and the contestants named, two more symbols might be decoded. Unfortunately, the choice of battles is rather wide and the dating of the stone far from certain. Some possibilities are listed below, with dates, from the Irish annals.

Nechtansmere (Duinnechtain, 686), well-known and decisive Pictish victory over Northumbrians fought not far from Aberlemno.
Monidcroib (possibly Moncrieff, 728), battle in Pictish civil war in which Oengus son of Fergus defeated Elpin.
Castle Credi (728), battle in Pictish civil war in which Oengus again defeated Elpin.
Monitcarno (729), battle in Pictish civil war in which Oengus defeated Nechtan.
Dromaderg blathmig (729), battle in Pictish civil war in which Oengus defeated Drust.
Possible battle (782), in which Dubhtollarg King of the Picts south of the Mounth

perished. If Dubhtollarg did die on the field of battle, the victor would have been Constantine son of Fergus.

Unnamed battle (789), in which Constantine defeated Conall mac Taidg and established himself as king of all the provinces of the Picts.

The Aberlemno church stone is not easy to date precisely, but is likely to be considerably later than the battle of Nechtansmere and, furthermore, if the triple disc symbol is to be associated with the vanquished army, then that army ought to be Pictish. The two most likely contenders for the notched rectangle and Z-rod symbol of the victor are Oengus son of Fergus in the first half of the eighth century and Constantine son of Fergus in the second half. Both fought battles during their rise to power, but the Irish annals document the earlier period much more fully than they do the later. It has to be admitted that a unique solution cannot yet be found for the Aberlemno church stone.

Oengus is also of interest in connection with symbols, because in 736 he invaded Dalriada, laid the country waste and took Dunadd, probably the most important fort in the whole country. On a rockface near the entrance to the fort is an incised carving of a boar, which is considered by some to be Pictish and therefore might have been carved as a symbol of the authority of Oengus. Against this correlation, however, the carving is likely to be much earlier than eighth century, and in any case is not a particularly 'Pictish' looking boar[6]. By analogy with the symbols carved at the entrance to Trusty's Hill, the Dunadd boar is perhaps more likely to be the symbol of a fifth-century Scottish king, perhaps an ally of Drust son of Erp, when the Picts and Scots were raiding southern Britain.

No other symbol stones, either by their position or by the scenes represented on them, suggest a possible historical association, and the interpretation of the symbols must remain correspondingly incomplete. The conclusions reached above may be summarized as follows:

1   The individual symbols, with a few important exceptions, represent personal names, just as in later centuries heraldic devices came to represent family names. In both cases the symbols served to identify an individual when he could not be seen, either because he was dead and buried or because he was totally encased in a suit of armour.

2   Readings for a few of these symbols have been suggested, as follows: double disc and Z-rod – Drust (Drosten); crescent and V-rod – Brude (Bridei); simple crescent – Ferat; 'tuning fork' – Nechtan.

3   The mirror, with or without comb, is interpreted as some sort of statement about the individual represented by the symbols being dead or buried or gone to heaven, and is an optional extra on gravestones.

4   The hammer and anvil is interpreted as manufacture in a broad sense, including building work.

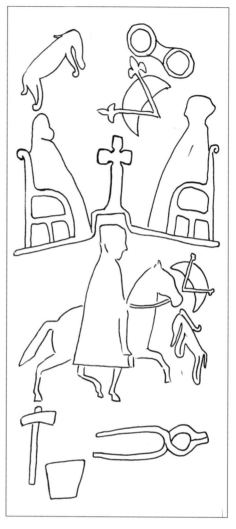

Cross slab at Dunfallandy (Perthshire). Left: reverse face, showing figures and Pictish symbols. The soft micaceous sandstone is rather weathered and the stone is protected from further damage by plate glass doors, which make photography (and even viewing) rather difficult. Right: diagrammatic representation of the essential elements on the reverse face.

In the *Pictish Chronicle* the kings are generally given what a biologist might call a binominal classification: they are identified by their own name plus a second name, which is generally the name of their father but might occasionally be a nickname. Thus we have Drust son of Erp, Drust son of Girom, Drust son of Wdrost, Drust son of Munait, Drust son of Talorgan and Drust son of Constantine, all distinguished by the names of their fathers. Quite apart from any parallels in the Welsh inscriptions, we might reasonably expect such a binominal classification to appear on the Pictish symbol stones. In view of the dominance of the two-symbol arrangement, it is reasonable to assume (but, by its very nature, almost impossible to prove) that the relationship 'son (or daughter) of' is implied between the two symbols of a pair.

Given the above conclusions, it is now possible to attempt a reading of a most unusual stone at Dunfallandy in Perthshire, which shows three figures (two seated and one on horseback) and no less than eight symbols. At the top left is a seated figure facing to the right with a Pictish 'elephant' symbol above his head. There is space for another symbol, but it seems to have been weathered away. At the top right is another seated figure facing to the left with a double disc above a crescent and V-rod. Between these two seated figures is a small free-standing cross. Beneath them is a third figure, on horseback, facing to the right with a crescent and V-rod above a Pictish 'elephant' symbol. Beneath the figure on horseback are the hammer and anvil, together with a pair of tongs.

If we let the 'elephant' symbol represent an imaginary name 'Dolphin', and for the double disc symbol we invent the name 'Doubledisc'; and if we also accept that the crescent and V-rod stands for Brude, and the hammer, anvil and tongs for manufacture or some related activity, we can now read the whole symbol sequence as follows:

[In memory of] Dolphin [son of] . . . [and] Doubledisc [daughter of] Brude, Brude son of Dolphin set up this cross.

There is no obvious distinction between the sexes of the two seated figures, except that the horseman and his (presumed) father are both facing to the right, whereas his (presumed) mother is facing to the left. But the system of naming is internally consistent. The upper symbol for the father is the same as the lower symbol for the son, as it should be if our interpretation is correct. Furthermore, the lower symbol for the mother is the same as the upper symbol for the son, which would mean that he was named after his maternal grandfather.

We do not have a Pictish equivalent of the Rosetta stone. Furthermore, the Ogham inscriptions found on a few symbol stones are no help because they are themselves virtually indecipherable. The Drosten stone is a very poor substitute and is likely to remain unique. What we need is to identify stones which, for one reason or another, can confidently be ascribed to particular historical events and known Pictish names. Most of the symbols are 'heraldic' in that they refer to the names of people; a few are hieroglyphic and represent words, actions or concepts. There is a gap of some four centuries between the last use of the Pictish symbols and the arrival of medieval heraldry, and there is no evidence of any continuity between the two.

CHAPTER 18

Sueno's Stone: into the Tenth Century

Sueno's stone is a magnificent cross slab, at 6.5 m (almost 22 feet) more than twice the height of any other Pictish cross. The shaft of the cross and the space on either side of it are covered by a remarkably uniform interlace pattern. The other face of the stone has a series of panels depicting details of a battle, with cavalry and foot soldiers, and the dead, beheaded and stacked one on top of the other, awaiting disposal. In one of the lower panels there is a curious scene showing a heap of bodies and their detached heads arranged under a sort of archway. This has been interpreted as a bridge[1], but might equally well be an illustration of mass burial under a large tumulus. There are no symbols on the stone and there is no inscription to aid in the interpretation of this great monument. A battle which was considered so important at the time is unlikely to have gone unrecorded. The only clues provided by the stone itself are its geographical location, its date and any significant details which might have been incorporated in the panels depicting the battle.

Sueno's stone is situated in the town of Forres, on the southern shore of the Moray Firth, between Elgin and Nairn. Its date is thought to be either ninth or tenth century. The cross face follows the tradition of the Pictish cross slabs, rather than the free-standing crosses of Ireland. The panels of figures, on the other hand, are much closer to tenth-century Irish crosses than to the freer style of the Pictish cross slabs. The dating by itself is not sufficiently precise to identify the battle, or even the likely contestants.

It has been suggested that the stone records the ultimate defeat of the Picts by Kenneth mac Alpin, though no such decisive battle was ever recorded, and the massacre at the banquet was hardly suitable subject-matter for such a great memorial. It could, on the other hand, commemorate a Picto–Scottish victory against the Vikings, or even a decisive battle in a Picto–Scottish civil war[2]. There are many battles to choose from during the two centuries in which Sueno's stone is likely to have been erected. The one clue which may throw some light on this problem is a traditional story about a great victory and a stone which was set up to commemorate it.

This story, which is linked to the ancient tradition about the Picts arriving

Sueno's stone, Forres (Moray). Left: cross face; right: reverse (narrative) face (Photos: Historic Scotland).

without any women of their own and eventually marrying Irish wives, is first found in Geoffrey of Monmouth's *Historia regum Brittaniae* and the equivalent Welsh language texts[3]. During the reign of a British king, Marius (Meurig), Roderic, King of the Picts, arrived from Scythia with a large fleet of ships and landed in northern Britain (Alban), which he proceeded to ravage and conquer. Marius quickly assembled an army and marched to meet the Picts. After much fighting he won a great victory, Roderic was slain, along with most of his army, and the rest were put to flight. In token of his triumph, Marius set up a great stone in the country called after him – Westymar, or, in Geoffrey's version, Westmorland. In most versions of the story the stone has an inscription on it to retain the memory of Marius for ever, but in Layamon's middle English version it is 'a most wonderful stone pillar' on which the king caused

> to be graven strange characters, of Rodrics death, and how he slew Rodric, and with horses drew him in pieces, and how he overcame the Peohtes [Picts] with his fight. Up he set the stone; yet it there standeth; so it will do as long as the world standeth[4].

The story then takes an unexpected turn. The survivors of the Pictish army submit themselves to Marius who, with quite astounding generosity, grants them the whole of Caithness to live in. Then comes the matter of the wives. Once they had settled in to their new territory, the Picts realized they were not going to make a go of it without any women, so they went to the Britons and asked for wives. Perhaps understandably the Britons would have nothing further to do with them, so they crossed over to Ireland and married Irish women, on condition, according to the Norman-French manuscript, 'that their issue should speak Irish, which language remains to this day in the Highlands among some who are called Scotch'[5].

Bede's story of the arrival of the Picts mentions no names and involves no battles. According to him the Picts arrived on the north coast of Ireland in a few longships, having sailed from Scythia and been driven round the coast of Britain by storms. They asked permission to settle, but there was not enough land available, so the Irish recommended that they should try the northern part of Britain. The Picts crossed the sea and, finding the Britons in possession of the south, settled in the north. They then asked the Irish for wives, and their request was granted, 'on condition that, when any dispute arose, they should choose a king from the female royal line rather than the male. This custom continues among the Picts to this day.'[6]

For some reason, by the twelfth century the battle between Marius and Roderic had become attached to the traditional story of how the first Picts came to take Irish wives. Why the two stories became joined in this way we do not know, but even without Bede's earlier authority the junction looks extremely artificial. So who were Marius and Roderic, and when and where did they fight their great battle?

Marius, in its Welsh form Meurig, was the name of a number of Welsh princes between the sixth and tenth centuries, but there is no particular reason to associate any of these men with the great battle against Roderic. Nor is there any good reason why Marius should be British or Roderic, for that matter, Pictish. These national attributions could simply be the result of attaching the story of the battle to the traditional tale about the Picts and their Irish wives. The fact that, in all versions of the story, the country where the battle took place was called Westymar (Westmorland, etc) after him makes one suspect that the name Marius was conjured up to provide an explanation for the name of the country. The name of Roderic is even less informative about the historical origin of the battle story.

More important than the names of the opposing kings are the names of places mentioned in the story. Geoffrey of Monmouth identifies Westymar with Westmorland, and later versions, building on this identification, state that the battle took place near Carlisle. Against this, all versions of the story agree that Roderic made his landfall in northern Britain and was causing trouble in Alban when Marius set out to meet him in battle. The other significant feature of the story is that the survivors of the Pictish army were granted Caithness to settle in. Caithness was an integral part of the Pictish kingdom, Cait being one of the seven legendary sons of Cruithne in the foundation story of the Picts. It was lost to the Vikings at about the end of the ninth century and became part of the Norse earldom of Orkney. The granting of Caithness to the 'Picts' by Marius is surely a reference to this loss of Caithness to the Norse settlers. If this is the correct interpretation of the story, then it fits in with the general dating of Sueno's stone and also with its geographical situation.

In the story of the battle, Marius set up his stone in a country called Westymar after his own name. The natural country to associate with the name Marius is Mar, roughly equivalent to the combined counties of Aberdeen and Buchan. Forres is actually situated in Moray, some distance west of Mar, though it could perhaps at one time have been referred to as being in Westymar. Taken all round, it seems highly probable that a memory of the erection of Sueno's stone is preserved in this story of Marius and his battle against Roderic and his Pictish army. No stone in the whole of Scotland has a greater claim to be remembered in folk tradition than Sueno's stone.

The evidence of the Irish annals is supplemented, for the period of the Viking invasions, by the 'Brechin Chronicle'[7], which contains a record of events from the reign of Kenneth mac Alpin to that of Kenneth son of Malcolm (841–995). Four invasions which might be compared with Roderic's attack are recorded in the chronicle, which gives us a Picto–Scottish view of the period.

In the seventh year of Kenneth mac Alpin (848–9) the Danes laid waste to Pictavia, as far as Clunie and Dunkeld. In the third year of Constantine son of Kenneth (865–6) Amlaebh (Olaf) and his people laid waste to Pictavia. This event is also recorded in the Irish annals, under the year 866. 'Amlaebh and Anisle went to Fortrenn with the Galls (foreigners) of Erin and Alban, and laid waste all Cruithentuaith, and carried off hostages.' The 'Brechin Chronicle' goes on to record another attack in the third year of the reign, in which Amlaebh was defeated by Constantine. But there must have been another attack a few years later, because the Irish annals record that in 871 'Amlaebh and Imar came again from Alban to Athcliath (Dublin), having a great number of prisoners, both

Britons and Albans and Saxons'[8]. There was yet another battle between the Danes and the Scots[9], at Dollar, in the fourteenth year of the reign (876–7). This was recorded in the Irish annals as between the Picts and the Dugalls (black foreigners). The final entry in the 'Brechin Chronicle' for this reign records the Norse plundering in Pictavia for a whole year.

The two sources, Picto–Scottish and Irish, are quite independent of one another. They often record different events and, when they record the same events, they record different aspects of them. Taking the two together, we can see no cause for celebration during the reign of Constantine son of Kenneth and no possible reason for setting up a great war memorial. From beginning to end the threat of further Viking attacks was never far away. The attacks continue in the following reigns.

Sometime during the reign of Donald son of Constantine (889–900), the Norse laid waste to Pictavia. There was also a battle at Innisibsolian between the Danes and the Scots, and another at Dunottar. Finally, in the third year of Constantine son of Aed (902–3), the Norse plundered Dunkeld and all Albania. In this instance the counter-attack is also recorded in the chronicle: in the following year (903–4) the Norse were slaughtered in Strathearn. In the Irish annals, under the year 904, we read that 'Ivor O'Ivor [was] slain by the men of Fortren, and great slaughter around him'.

Strathearn in Perthshire is a far remove from Forres, but from this time on there is no further mention of the Vikings penetrating into the heart of the country. What seems to have been the decisive battle in the long campaign against the Vikings passed without notice in the 'Brechin Chronicle' and the *Annals of Ulster*, but it is recorded in some detail under the year 909 in the version of the Irish annals transcribed by Duald MacFirbis[10].

Almost at the same time, the men of Fortrenn and the Lochlanns [Vikings] fought a battle. Vigorously, indeed, did the men of Alban fight this battle, for Columcille [St Columba] was assisting them, for they prayed to him fervently, because he was their apostle, and it was through him they had received the faith. On a former occasion, when Imhar Conung was a young man, he came to plunder Alban with three large battalions. What the men of Alban, both laity and clergy, did, was to remain until morning fasting and praying to God and to Columcille, and they cried aloud to the Lord, and gave many alms of food and clothes to the churches and to the poor, and to take the body of the Lord from the hands of the priests, and to promise to do every good as their clergy would order them; and they would have as their standard at the head of every battle the crozier of Columcille, for which reason it was called Cathbhuaith from the time forth; and this was a befitting name for it, for they have often gained victory in battles by means of it, as they did afterwards at that time when they put their trust in Columcille. They acted in the same way on this occasion. This battle was afterwards fought fiercely and vigorously. The Albanich [men of Alban] gained victory and triumph. The Lochlanns were slain in great numbers and defeated, and their king was slain, viz., Otter, son of Iargna; and it was long after this until either Danes or Lochlanns attacked them, but they enjoyed peace and tranquillity.

Here at last was a decisive victory. Never again does the 'Brechin Chronicle' mention Danish or Norse raiders penetrating into the heart of the country. The Irish annalist was right when he said that the battle heralded an era of peace and tranquillity. After the battle it is probable that the Vikings were forced to sign a treaty of non-aggression, in return for which Constantine recognized the reality of Norse rule in Caithness and gave up any claims he may have had to that province.

After a century of Viking attacks, such a victory and such a treaty, such peace and tranquillity, would be cause for celebration indeed. The erection of a magnificent monument to commemorate the great battle would have been entirely appropriate. The traditional story of the great battle between Marius and Roderic, the annalists' account of Constantine's great victory over the Vikings, and the erection of Sueno's stone all come together in an interpretation of this period of history. Official recognition of the loss of Caithness is equivalent to the granting of that county to the survivors of Roderic's defeated army. Even Otter, the Viking king who was slain in the battle, may have been the real-life model for Roderic of the story; the names are not unlike.

But who were the victors? Were they the Picts, in whose chronicle the Viking raids were recorded? Were they the men of Fortren, the men of Alban or the Albanich, all mentioned in the annalist's account of the battle, or were they the Scots? And what country did they free from the threat of Viking raids? Was it Pictavia or Albania, both mentioned in the 'Brechin Chronicle' of the period, was it Cruithentuaith, as in the Irish annals for 871, or was it Scotia or Scotland?

The answer is that they were all of these, for they were but different names applied to the same people and their country at different times. Indeed Constantine in his long life spanned the complete range of this terminological jungle. When his father, Aed son of Kenneth mac Alpin, died in 878, his obituary notice in the Irish annals referred to him as King of the Picts. Constantine came to the throne in 900, after the death of his cousin Donald, who was described as King of Alban. Constantine reigned for 40 years and, in the thirty-fourth year of his reign, fought in the battle of Duinbrunde, where his son was killed. The Irish annals, under the year 937, describe this as a battle between the Saxons and the Norsemen, and make no mention of the Picts or Scots, or the men of Fortren or Alban. Both sides suffered great losses, but Athelstan, King of the Saxons, won a great victory and Olaf, the Norse king, made his escape with a few followers. This was the battle of Brunanburh, well known from the *Anglo-Saxon Chronicle* and a contemporary Old English poem, in which an English army under the leadership of Athelstan, King of Wessex, won a decisive victory over the Norsemen. Constantine, 'King of the Scots', was fighting on the Norse side and the *Anglo-Saxon Chronicle*, like the 'Brechin Chronicle', records the death of his son.

After a reign of 40 years, Constantine handed over to his cousin, Malcolm son of Donald, and joined the Culdees at St Andrews, where he was abbot for 5 years and eventually died in 952. He was son of the last recorded King of the Picts, and was himself known as King of Alban by the Irish and as King of the Scots by the English. If anyone deserved the title of first King of the Scots, that person was surely Constantine son of Aed. Earlier kings, Constantine's grandfather Kenneth mac Alpin included, were only known as kings of the Scots retrospectively. With Constantine's long life, the age of the Picts came to an end and the age of the Scots began. The metamorphosis was complete. Without recourse to the legendary genocide, the Picts had simply become the Scots: no revolution, no murders at the banquet, no change of dynasty or government.

The process had begun with the union of the kingdoms, first under Constantine son of Fergus at the very beginning of the ninth century, and later under Kenneth mac Alpin. As a result of this union, the Scottish kingdom of Dalriada became the county of Argyll, one of the provinces of the Picts. The Scots of Dalriada became in effect Picts, or men of Fortren. This enlarged Pictish kingdom went through a century of harrowing raids by the Vikings, during which it gradually lost control of the old Pictish province of Caithness. The nation which emerged, bruised but intact, into the tenth century was the new kingdom of Scotland. The change of name, for it was nothing more, provides a convenient label for the passage from one age to the next.

APPENDIX 1

The *Pictish Chronicle*: Group A and Group B Compared

For detailed discussion, see Chapter 3.

GROUP A (971–5, 1040–72)		GROUP B (1187, 1251, 1280, 1317)	
Name	Reign (years)	Name	Reign (years)
1 Gud	50, 100 or 150	Gede	50, 100 or 150
2 Tharain	100	Tharan	100
3 Morleo	15		
4 Deocilunon	40	Duchil	40
5 Cimoiod son of Arcois	7		
6 Deoord	50	Deordegele	20
7 Bliesblituth	5		
8 Deototreic brother of Diu	40	Derothet	60
9 Usconbuts	20	Combust	20
10 Crautreic	40	Karanthrecht	40
11 Deordivois	20		
12 Uist	50		
13 Ru	100		
14 Gartnait bolc	4		
15 Gartnait ini	9	Gernarg bolg	9
16 Breth son of Buthut	7		
17 Vipoig namet	30	Vipogwenech	30
18		Fiacha albus	30
19 Canutulachama	4	Cantulmet	6
20		Dornornauch nerales	1
21 Wradech uecla	2	Feradech finlegh	2
22 Gartnaich diuberr	60	Garnard dives	60
23 Talore son of Achivir	75	Talarg son of Keother	25
24 Drust son of Erp	100	Drust son of Irb	100
25 Talore son of Aniel	4	Tholarg son of Anile	2
26 Necton morbet son of Erip	24	Nectan celchamoth	10
27 Drest Gurthinmoch	30	Drust gocinecht	30
28 Galanan erilich	12	Galany	15

Name	Reign (years)	Name	Reign (years)
29 Drest son of Gyrom and		Drust son of Gurum	5
30 Drest son of Wdrost		Drust son of Hudrossig	8
(together)	5		
31 Drest son of Girom (alone)	5	Drust son of Gurum	4
32 Garthnac son of Girom	7	Ganat son of Gigurum	6
33 Cailtran son of Girom	1	Kelturan his brother	6
34 Talorg son of Muircholaich	11	Tolorg son of Mordeleg	11
35 Drest son of Munait	1	Drust son of Moneth	1
36 Galam cennaleph	4	Tagaled	4
37 with Bridei	1		
38 Bridei son of Mailcon	30	Brude son of Melcho	30
39 Gartnait son of Domnach	11	Gernard son of Dompneth	20
40 Nectan nephew or		Nathad son of Irb	21
grandson of Uerb	20		
41 Cinioch son of Lutrin	19	Kinet son of Luthren	14 or 24
42 Gartnait son of Wid	5	Nectan son of Fochle	5 or 8
43 Breidei son of Wid	5	Brude son of Fochle	5
44 Talore their brother	12	Tolarg son of Fethar	11
45 Tallorcen son of Enfret	4	Talargan son of Anfrud	4
46 Gartnait son of Donnel	6½	Garnarth son of Donnal	5
47 Drest his brother	7	Drust his brother	6
48 Bredei son of Bili	21	Brude son of Bile	21
49 Taran son of Entifidich	4	Taran son of Amfredech	14
50 Bredei son of Derelei	11	Brude son of Derili	31
51 Necthon son of Derelei	10 or 15	Nectan his brother	18
52		Carnach son of Ferach	24
53		Oengus son of Fergus	16
54		Nectan son of Derili	9 months
55		Oengus son of Brude	6 months
56 Drest and		Alpin son of Engus	8
57 Elpin (together)	5	Drust son of Talorgen	5
58 Onnist son of Urguist	30	Hungus son of Fergus	10
59 Bredei son of Wirguist	2 or 15		
60		Engus son of Brude	36
61		Brude son of Engus	2
62		Alpin son of Engus	8
63 Ciniod son of Wredech	12		
64 Elpin son of Wroid	3½		
65 Drest son of Talorgen	1	Drust son of Talorgen	1
66 Talorcan son of Drostan	4 or 5	Talorgan son of Drustan	4
67 Talorgen son of Onnist	2½ or 12½	Talargan son of Engus	5
68 Canaul son of Tarl'a	5		
69 Constantin son of Wrguist	35	Constantinus son of Fergus	42
70 Unnuist son of Wrguist	12	Hungus son of Fergus	10
71 Drest son of Constantin and			
72 Talorgen son of Wthoil			
(together)	3	Drustalorg	4
73 Uven son of Unuist	3	Eogana son of Hungus	3
74 Wrad son of Bargoit	3	Ferach son of Bacoc	3
75 and Bred	1	Brude son of Ferech	1
76		Kineth son of Ferech	1
77		Brude son of Fokel	2
78		Drust son of Ferach	3
79 Kinadius son of Alpin	16	Kinart son of Alpin	16

APPENDIX 2

The *Pictish Chronicle*: Calibration

The following lists indicate the length of each reign, followed by the Pictish dates (taking the death of Brude son of Maelchon as 584 and adding the successive reign lengths), the Irish dates for the end of each reign (taken from the annals) and finally the error (plus if the Irish dates are greater, minus if they are less).

KING LIST (971–95)

Name	Reign (years)	Pictish dates	Irish dates	Error
Breidei son of Mailcon	30	554–84	584	0
Gartnait son of Domnach	11	584–95	599	+4
Nectan nepos Uerb	20	595–615		
Cinioch son of Lutrin	19	615–34	631	−3
Gartnait son of Wid	5	634–9	635	−4
Breidei son of Wid	5	639–44	641	−3
Talore son of Wid	12	644–56	653	−3
Tallorcen son of Enfret	4	656–60	657	−3
Gartnait son of Donnel	6½	660–6	663	−3
Drest son of Donnel	7	666–73	672	−1
Bredei son of Bili	21	673–94	693	−1
Taran son of Entifidich	4	694–8	697	−1
Bredei son of Derelei	11	698–709	706	−3
Necthon son of Derelei	15	709–24	726	+2
Drest and Elpin	5	724–9	728	−1
Onnist son of Urguist	30	729–59	761	+2
Bredei son of Wirguist	2	759–61	763	+2
Ciniod son of Wredech	12	761–73	775	+2
Elpin son of Wroid	3½	773–7	780	+3
Drest son of Talorgen	1	777–8		
Talorgen son of Drest	4 or 5	778–82		
Talorgen son of Onnist	2½	782–5		

Canaul son of Tarl'a	5	785–90	789	–1
Constantin son of Wrguist	35	790–825	820	–5
Unnuist son of Wrguist	12	825–37	834	–3
Drest son of Constantin and				
Talorgen son of Wthoil	3	837–40		
Uven son of Unuist	3	840–3		
Wrad son of Bargoit	3	843–6		
Bred	1	846–7		
Kinadius son of Alpin	16	847–3	858	–5

The correlation between the earliest version of the *Pictish Chronicle* and the dates recorded in the Irish annals is remarkable. Over a period of three hundred years, the difference between the Pictish and Irish dates is never greater than 5 years either way. As a guide to chronology, this version of the *Pictish Chronicle* is thus shown to be thoroughly reliable back to the middle of the sixth century.

KING LIST (1317)

Name	Reign (years)	Pictish dates	Irish dates	Error
Brude son of Melcho	30	554–84	584	0
Gernard son of Dompnath	20	584–604	599	–5
Nathad son of Irb	21	604–25		
Kinet son of Luthren	14	625–39	631	–8
Nectan son of Fochle	8	639–47		
Brude son of Fochle	5	647–52	641	–11
Tolarg son of Fethar	11	652–63	653	–10
Talargan son of Anfrud	4	663–7	657	–10
Garnarth son of Donnal	5	667–72	663	–9
Drust son of Donnal	6	672–8	672	–6
Brude son of Bile	21	678–99	693	–6
Taran son of Amfredech	14	699–713	697	–6
Brude son of Derili	31	713–44	706	–38
Nectan son of Derili	18	744–62	724	–38
Carnach son of Ferach	24	762–86		
Oengus son of Fergus	16	786–802		
Nectan son of Derili	9 months	802–3	732	–71
Oengus son of Brude	6 months	803–3		
Alpin son of Engus	8 years*	803–11	728	–83
Drust son of Talorgen	1	811–12		
Hungus son of Fergus	10*	812–22	761	–61
Engus son of Brude	36	822–58		
Brude son of Engus	2	858–60		
Alpin son of Engus	8*	860–8		
Drust son of Talorgen	1	868–9		
Taloran son of Drustan	4	869–73		

Talargan son of Engus	5	873–8	
Constantinus son of Fergus	42	878–920	820	−100
Hungus son of Fergus	10*	920–30	834	−96
Drustalorg	4	930–4	
Eogana son of Hungus	3	934–7	
Ferach son of Bacoc	3	937–40	
Brude son of Ferech	1	940–1	
Kineth son of Ferech	1	941–2	
Brude son of Fokel	2	942–4	
Drust son of Ferach	3	944–7	
Kinart son of Alpin	16	947–63	858	−105

This list shows a very poor correlation with the dates provided by the Irish annals. At the end of the same three-hundred-year period the Pictish dates are in error by over a hundred years. Throughout the whole period the errors are in the same direction. The timescale indicated by this list is consistently too long. For one reason or another many of the reign lengths must have been overestimated; others may have been duplicated (indicated by *). The list is not without historical interest, but as a guide to chronology it is worse than useless.

The Mystery of the Thirty Brudes: a Pre-Pictish Memory

A unique feature of the group A version of the *Pictish Chronicle* is the statement about the thirty kings, all called Brude, who ruled over Hibernia (Ireland) and Albania (Scotland) for 150 years. The names of these kings (actually only twenty-eight of them) occur in pairs, as shown below, and, unlike all the other kings in the list, they do not have individual reign lengths. They form a distinct unit in the *Pictish Chronicle*, situated several generations after the sons of Cruithne and immediately before Gede (Gilgidi), who heads the main list of kings in all versions of the chronicle (see Appendix 1).

Brude Pant	Brude Urpant
Brude Leo	Brude Urleo
Brude Gant	Brude Urgant
Brude Gnith	Brude Urgnith
Brude Fecir	Brude Urfecir
Brude Cal	Brude Urcal
Brude Cint	Brude Urcint
Brude Fec	Brude Urfec
Brude Ru	Brude Urru
Brude Gart	Brude Urgart
Brude Cinid	Brude Urcnid
Brude Uip	Brude Uruip
Brude Grid	Brude Urgrid
Brude Mund	Brude Urmund

These Brudes are most unlikely to have been genuine early kings and equally unlikely to be fictional names invented for the purpose of lengthening the list at some later date. In either case we would expect individual reign lengths to be given, as in the rest of the list, and we would not expect such a strange assortment of name pairs. We can only conclude that the Brude pairs, when first set down in the *Pictish Chronicle*, were already in existence in the oral tradition but had lost their original meaning. It was then presumed that they must have been the names of long-forgotten kings. If they were not early kings and are not later additions, what are they?

Some light is shed on the problem by the pedigree of the kings of Gwynedd,[1] whose ancestor Cunedda came south from Manau Gododdin with his eight sons to drive the Irish out of North Wales. In the pedigree, Cunedda is the son of Oetern (Eternus), son of Patern Pesrud (Paternus of the red tunic), son of Tacit (Tacitus), son of Cein, son of Guorcein, son of Doli, son of Guordoli, son of Dumn, son of Guordumn, son of Amguoloyt, son of Anguerit, son of Oumun, son of Dubun, son of Brithguein, son of Eugein, son of Aballac, son of Amalech, son of Beli the Great and Anna, 'who they say was the cousin of Mary the Virgin, mother of our Lord Jesus Christ'. There are no Brudes in this pedigree, but there can be no doubt about the similarity of the three 'name pairs' shown below to the Brude pairs in the *Pictish Chronicle*.

Cein	Guorcein
Doli	Guordoli
Dumn	Guordumn

In both lists, the *Pictish Chronicle* and the Welsh genealogy, the simple member of the pair appears before the compound member. This provides further evidence that these are not the names of kings. The *Pictish Chronicle* is a list of kings, starting with the earliest. Thus the simple member of each pair (e.g. Brude Pant) is earlier than the compound member (e.g. Brude Urpant). The Welsh genealogy, on the other hand, starts with the most recent kings and proceeds backwards from son to father. Thus the simple member of each pair (e.g. Cein) is later than the compound member (e.g. Guorcein). In both documents the name pairs have been added without any real understanding of their meaning.

In the Welsh genealogy the Pictish prefix *Ur* has been replaced by *Guor*, an early Welsh form of *ver* meaning 'over'. Thus Vertigern, an earlier form of the familiar Vortigern (over lord or high lord), appears in the Latin text of Nennius as *Guorthigernus*. Pictish names behave in a similar way. The well-known name Fergus (sometimes spelt Forgus) appears in the group A version of the *Pictish Chronicle* as Urguist. The Gaelic *for* has the same meaning as *ver*.[2]

The genealogy of the Scottish kings, as set down for William the Lion,[3] also has similar name pairs. If we go back fifteen generations from Echdach-riada we come to Sin, son of Rosin, son of Their, son of Rotheir. Going back a further sixty-two generations we come to Goildilgleis (Gaidelus), and after another seven generations to Agmemnon. Thirteen generations further back is Gomer son of Jafeth, son of Noah, and so on to Adam, son of the living God. As in the Welsh pedigree, there are no Brudes here, but the name pairs look familiar.

Sin	Rosin
Their	Rotheir

Here the Pictish *ur* has become *ro*, a Gaelic 'intensive' meaning 'very' or 'too', so that whatever Sin may have meant, Rosin was more so. In these name pairs the prefixes *ur*, *guor* and *ro* all have very similar meanings and somehow add emphasis, making the compound word greater than the simple one that precedes it.

The five lists are quite unlike each other. The Welsh genealogy is much shorter than the *Pictish Chronicle*, while the Scottish genealogy is much longer. The only thing they have in common is the presence of these distinctive name pairs. It is therefore probable that the name pairs are fragments derived from an ancient oral tradition, a tradition preceding the development of a Pictish national consciousness, preceding the emergence of the Scottish kingdom of Dalriada, and long preceding Cunedda's migration to North Wales.

The unique feature of the Pictish name pairs is that they are all set out as nicknames or descriptive names, enabling us to distinguish between a long line of kings who were all called Brude. Brude (Bridei) is a well-known Pictish name, but thirty in unbroken succession would stretch our credulity to breaking point. These cannot be the names of kings. If we now consider Brude as a word, rather than a name, the old Welsh *brud* (*brut*), meaning a prophecy or chronicle, immediately suggests itself. If, as suggested in Chapter 2, the king lists were recited in public at great national festivals, it is likely that the name pairs found their way into the oral tradition by the same route. If they are not the names of kings, then what are they? Perhaps they are most likely to be the deeds of the kings, or possibly the attributes or extent of their kingdom. It would be unwise to attempt an interpretation of each individual name pair, but if we suppose that in the first pair of Brudes the word *pant* means a valley, as in modern Welsh, we may be able to see how the name pairs worked.

At a recognized stage in the proceedings, the master of ceremonies (high priest or chief bard, perhaps) would recite a list of all the rich valleys in the kingdom, at the end of which he would call out '*Brude Pant*' (valley chronicle). The assembled people would then respond with a great shout of '*Brude Urpant*' (great valley chronicle), thus capping the first call and expressing their pride in their corporate identity. The master of ceremonies would then proceed with the next recitation and call out '*Brude Leo*', upon which the crowd would shout back '*Brude Urleo*'. And so on. We may never know the precise meaning of the individual name pairs, but crowd responses provide an explanation of their general character.

Notes

Chapter 1

1 F.T. Wainwright, 'The Picts and the Problem', in: F.T. Wainwright (ed.), *The Problem of the Picts*, Edinburgh, Thomas Nelson, 1956, p. 13

2 J.G.P. Friell and W.G. Watson (eds), *Pictish Studies: Settlements, Burial and Art in Dark Age Northern Britain*, British Archaeological Reports, 125, Oxford, 1984; A. Small (ed.), *The Picts: A New Look at some Old Problems*, Dundee, 1987

3 T. Watkins, 'Where were the Picts: An Essay in Settlement Achaeology', in: J.G.P. Friell and W.G. Watson (eds), *Pictish Studies: Settlement, Burial and Art in Dark Age Northern Britain*, British Archaeological Reports, 125, Oxford, 1984, p. 83

4 L. Alcock, 'Pictish Studies: Present and Future', in: Small 1987, pp. 80ff.

5 Ibid., p. 91

6 Ibid, p. 92

7 L. Sherley-Price (trs.), *Bede: Ecclesiastical History of the English People with Bede's Letter to Egbert and Cuthbert's Letter on the Death of Bede*, rev. edn, Harmondsworth, Penguin, 1990, pp. 41–3

8 Ibid., p. 45

9 Ibid., p. 46

10 Ibid., p. 148

Chapter 2

1 Sherley-Price, 1900, p. 148

2 W.F. Skene (ed.), *Chronicles of the Picts, Chronicles of the Scots, and other Early Memorials of Scottish History*, HM General Register House, Edinburgh, 1867, pp. 4–10, 24–30, 396–400

3 Ibid., p. 4

4 Ibid., p. 322. In the phrase 'as the poet says', the poet is sometimes Columcille (St Columba) and sometimes the wise man (ibid, p. 25)

5 Ibid., pp. ciii–civ; Wainwright, 1956, pp. 46–7; I. Henderson, *The Picts*, London, Thames and Hudson, 1967, pp. 35–6

6 Skene, 1867, p. 136

7 Ibid., p. 135

8 A.W. Wade-Evans (ed. and trs.), *Nennius: History of the Britons etc.*, London, Church Historical Society, 1938, pp. 101–2

9 G.N. Garmonsway (trs.), *Anglo-Saxon Chronicle*, London, Dent, 1953

10 Skene, 1867, pp. 30, 33, 122–3, 159–60, 298, 319, 322, 329

11 Ibid., p. 329

12 R.G. Collingwood and J.N.L. Myers, *Roman Britain and the English Settlements*, 2nd edn, Oxford, Clarendon Press, 1937, p. 31

13 C.H. Oldfather (trs.), *Diodorus of Sicily*, Vol. III, London, Heinemann, 1939, pp. 151–9

14 A. Macbain, 'Ptolomey's Geography of Scotland', *Transactions of the Gaelic Society of Inverness*, XVIII (1892), 267–88

Chapter 3

1 Skene, 1867, pp. 7, 28, 399

2 Ibid., p. 8

3 Ibid., pp. 4–10, 24–30, 149–52, 172–6, 200–8, 285–90, 396–400

4 Ibid., pp. lii–liii, lv–lvi, lviii–lix, lxv

5 Ibid., pp. xix, lv–lvi

6 The spelling of Pictish names is a matter of some difficulty. There was certainly no contemporary standard spelling and they would have been written down phonetically.

The result for any given name varied according to the date, place and language (generally Pictish, Gaelic or Latin) of writing. Thus Pictish 'Wrguist' is equivalent to Gaelic 'Fergus'; 'Bridei', 'Bredei', Bruide' and 'Brude' are all equivalent; as are 'Talorgan', 'Talorcen', 'Tollargen', etc. In order to avoid confusion, such relatively common names have been standardized (except in direct quotations from sources)

7   Skene, 1867, pp. cxxiii–cxxvi
8   Ibid., p. clxxxviii
9   Ibid., pp. cxxiv–cxxvi
10 Henderson, 1967, pp. 96–7
11 Sherley-Price, 1990, p. 148
12 Ibid., p. 308
13 Skene, 1867, pp. 66–78, 343–74

Chapter 4

1   Skene, 1867, pp. 66–78, 343–74, gives extracts of the entries relevant to the history of Scotland. There is so much in common between these two annals that an earlier lost source is believed to have existed. This 'Ulster Chronicle' may have been written in Iona (M.O. Anderson, *Kings and Kingship in Early Scotland*, Edinburgh and London, Scottish Academic Press, 1980, pp. 1–42)
2   Wainwright, 1956, p. 148
3   Sherley-Price, 1990, p. 148
4   Skene, 1867, p. 6
5   Ibid., pp. 6, 28, 399

Chapter 5

1   M. Winterbottom (ed. and trs.), *Gildas: The Ruin of Britain and Other Works*, London, Phillimore, 1978, pp. 28–36
2   L. Thorpe (trs.), *Geoffrey of Monmouth: The History of the Kings of Britain*, London, Penguin, 1966, p. 75
3   W.A. Cummins, *King Arthur's Place in Prehistory: The Great Age of Stonehenge*, Stroud, Alan Sutton Publishing, 1992, Chapter 2
4   F.M. Stenton, *Anglo-Saxon England*, 2nd edn, Oxford, Clarendon Press, 1947, pp. 33–5
5   S. Frere, *Britannia: A History of Roman Britain*, London, Routledge and Kegan Paul, 3rd edn, 1987, Chapter 5
6   M. Hutton (trs.), *Tacitus in Five Volumes*, Vol. 1, Pt 1, 'Agricola', London, Heinemann, 1980, p. 97

7   Ibid., p. 77
8   Frere, 1987, pp. 147–8
9   E. Cary (trs.), *Dio's Roman History*, Vol. 9, London, Heinemann, 1927, p. 263
10 Frere, 1987, Chapter 8
11 Henderson, 1967, Chapter 1
12 Skene, 1867, pp. 357, 358
13 R.E.M. Wheeler, *Maiden Castle, Dorset*, Report of the Research Committee of the Society of Antiquaries of London, XII, 1943

Chapter 6

1   A.H. Williams, *An Introduction to the History of Wales*, Vol. 1: *Prehistoric Times to 1063 AD*, Cardiff, University of Wales Press, 1941, pp. 159–60
2   Wainwright, 1956, p. 28
3   Ibid., 1956, p. 27
4   Cary, 1927, p. 263
5   Henderson, 1967, p. 32
6   Wainwright, 1956, p. 27
7   Ibid., p. 25
8   Sherley-Price, 1990, pp. 143–4
9   Ibid., p. 144
10 Skene, 1867, pp. 408–9
11 Doubt has recently been cast on the baptism of Brude, because it is not recorded in Adomnan's life of St Columba (L. Laing and J. Laing, *The Picts and the Scots*, Stroud, Alan Sutton Publishing, 1973, pp. 24, 49). The relationship between Brude son of Maelchon and St Columba, and the evidence of Adomnan's life of the saint, are discussed in detail in Chapter 11
12 J. Morris, *The Age of Arthur: A History of the British Isles from 350–650*, London, Weidenfeld and Nicolson, 1973, p. 192
13 Winterbottom, 1978, pp. 32–6
14 Skene, 1867, pp. ci–ciii
15 A.P. Smyth, *Warlords and Holy Men: Scotland AD 80–1000*, London, Edward Arnold, 1984, pp. 71–2. An interesting comparison is made with the kings of Leinster, for whom tribal king lists and genealogies also survive

Chapter 7

1   Wainwright, 1956, p. 11
2   Ibid., p. 15
3   W.F.H. Nicolaisen, *Scottish Place-names: Their Study and Significance*, London, Batsford, 1976, Chapter 3

4 K.H. Jackson, 'The Pictish Language', in: Wainwright, 1956, pp. 146–8; Nicolaisen, 1976, pp. 151–8

5 Nicolaisen, 1976, p. 156

6 Ibid, pp. 154–6

7 Ibid., pp. 39–46

8 Ibid., p. 45

9 Ibid., Chapter 5

10 Ibid., Chapter 6

11 Sherley-Price, 1990, p. 59

12 Nicolaisen, 1976, p. 165

13 Jackson, 1956, p. 131

14 Nicolaisen, 1976, p. 132

15 A.O. Anderson and M.O. Anderson (eds and trs), *Adomnan's Life of St Columba*, London, Thomas Nelson, 1961, pp. 275, 397

16 K.H. Jackson, 'Common Gaelic: The Evolution of the Goedelic Languages', *Proceedings of the British Academy*, Vol. XXXVII (1951)

17 Ibid., p. 93

18 Wainwright, 1956, pp. 40–4

19 Hutton, 1980, p. 47

Chapter 8

1 Skene, 1867, pp. 135–6; J.B. Johnston, *Place-names of Scotland*, Edinburgh, David Douglas, 1892

2 Sherley-Price, 1990, p. 46. It should be noted that Bede's word *Scotti* is translated as 'Irish' in this edition

3 Ibid., p. 96

4 Skene, 1867, pp. 133–4, 144–5

5 Anderson and Anderson, 1961, p. 36

6 Skene, 1867, p. 145

7 Ibid., p. 195

8 J. Morris (ed. and trs.), *Nennius: British History and the Welsh Annals*, London, Phillimore, 1980, p. 21

9 C. Renfrew, *British Prehistory: A New Outline*, London, Duckworth, 1974, pp. 11–19

10 Skene, 1867, pp. 57–64

11 D. West (trs.), *Virgil: The Aeneid*, London, Penguin, 1990, p. 3

12 Ibid., p. 158

13 Morris, 1980, p. 19

14 Thorpe, 1966, p. 75

15 Skene, 1867, p. 17

16 Anderson, 1980, p. 135

17 Anderson and Anderson, 1961, p. 461

18 Anderson, 1980, p. 106

19 Anderson and Anderson, 1961, p. 461

20 Ibid., p. 409

21 Ibid., pp. 245, 459

22 Anderson, 1980, p. 135

23 Hutton, 1980, pp. 97–9

24 V.E. Nash-Williams, *The Early Christian Monuments of Wales*, Cardiff, University of Wales Press, 1950, p. 107

25 A. Ritchie and D.J. Breeze, *Invaders of Scotland*, Edinburgh, HMSO, 1991, p. 19 and back cover

Chapter 9

1 Skene, 1867, pp. 4–10, 24–30, 396–400. The additional information about the later kings, from Kenneth mac Alpin onwards, in the 971–95 version are not found in the others and must have been incorporated from some other source

2 Ibid., p. 18

3 See Chapter 4, p. 30

4 Skene, 1867, p. 152

5 Ibid., pp. 6, 28, 399

6 Anderson, 1980, p. 84

7 Ibid., pp. 92–3

8 Sherley-Price, 1990, p. 148

9 See Chapters 3 and 4

10 Skene, 1867, p. 173

11 Ibid., p. 150

12 Ibid., p. 201

13 Ibid., p. 286

14 Sherley-Price, 1990, p. 148

15 W.M. Metcalfe, *The Legends of SS Ninian and Malchor, from an Unique MS in the Scottish Dialect of the Fourteenth Century*, Paisley, Alexander Gardner, 1904, pp. 187–209

16 W.M. Metcalfe, *Pinkerton's Lives of the Scottish Saints*, rev. edn, Vol. II, Paisley, Alexander Gardner, 1889, p. 23

17 Ibid., p. 58

18 Wainright, 1956, pp. 40–4

19 Anderson and Anderson, 1961, p. 441

20 Symbols carved on a rock outcrop near the entrance to the hill-fort known as Trusty's Hill, near Gatehouse of Fleet

21 Smyth, 1984, p. 82

22 Skene, 1867, p. 6

23 For this last phase of the history of Roman Britain, see Frere, 1987, Chapter 16

24 Sherley-Price, 1990, pp. 69–70

Chapter 10

1 L. Alcock, *Arthur's Britain: History and Archaeology*, London, Penguin, 1971, p. 254

2 Morris, 1980, p. 37

3 Wade Evans, 1938, p. 113

4   Williams, 1941, p. 70
5   Collingwood and Myres, 1937, p. 289;
    Alcock, 1971, pp. 125–9
6   Morris, 1980, p. 35; Thorpe, 1966, p. 215
7   R.B.K. Stevenson, 'Pictish Chain, Roman
    Silver and Bauxite Beads', *Proceedings of the
    Society of Antiquaries of Scotland*, 88 (1956),
    228–30
8   The date of deposition of the Norrie's Law
    hoard is still controversial. J. Graham-
    Campbell, 'Norrie's Law, Fife: On the
    Nature and Dating of the Silver Hoard',
    *Proceedings of the Society of Antiquaries of
    Scotland*, 121 (1991), 241–59 concluded
    that 'it was deposited most probably during
    the second half of the seventh century',
    whereas Laing and Laing (1993, pp.
    112–15) considered that 'a seventh century
    deposition of the hoard would be very
    difficult to support'. The late date is based
    entirely on the artistic style of the symbols
    engraved on the leaf-shaped plaques, in
    particular a comparison between the
    animal's head and various heads depicted in
    the early eighth-century Lindisfarne
    Gospels. The similarity is a matter of
    opinion, and Graham-Campbell himself
    admitted that 'there is no way in which the
    plaques may be dated precisely'. Without
    such dating, the case for a seventh-century
    deposition of the Norrie's Law hoard has no
    foundation. An early starting date for
    incised Pictish symbols, though difficult to
    prove, has some support (L. Laing and J.
    Laing, 'The Date and Origin of the Pictish
    Symbols', *Proceedings of the Society of
    Antiquaries of Scotland*, 114 (1984), 261–76
9   J. Close-Brooks, 'Excavations at Clatchard
    Craig, Fife', *Proceedings of the Society of
    Antiquaries of Scotland*, 116 (1986), 117–84
10 A.C. Thomas, 'Excavations at Trusty's Hill,
    Anwoth, 1960', *Transactions of the Dumfries
    and Galloway Natural History and
    Archaeological Society*, 38 (1961), 58–70
11 Alcock, 1971, pp. 161–2. Related names in
    the south-west are Bartrostan (NX 380595),
    south of Newton Stewart, and Troston (NX
    923687), south of Dumfries. Both are
    relatively early names, after which other
    features (Bartrostan Burn and Troston Hill)
    are named
12 Frere, 1987, p. 101
13 D. Dumville *et al.*, *Saint Patrick, AD
    493–1993*, Woodbridge, Boydell Press,
    1993, p. 108

Chapter 11

1   Sherley-Price, 1990, p. 148
2   Skene, 1867, pp. 67, 344, 345
3   Anderson and Anderson, 1961, p. 441
4   Ibid., p. 259
5   Ibid., p. 279
6   Ibid., pp. 397, 399
7   Ibid., p. 493
8   Smyth, 1984, p. 102
9   Anderson and Anderson, 1961, p. 409
10 Ibid., p. 185
11 Ibid., p. 461
12 Smyth, 1984, p. 105
13 Anderson and Anderson, 1961, p. 409
14 See Chapter 4. It is evident from
    subsequent events that the Parts A and B of
    the Pictish Kingdom, suggested in that
    chapter, are respectively the Southern and
    Northern Picts
15 Anderson and Anderson, 1961, p. 403
16 Ibid., pp. 469, 471
17 Ibid., pp. 223, 225

Chapter 12

1   Sherley-Price, 1990, p. 97
2   Ibid., pp. 126–8
3   Ibid., p. 134
4   Ibid., p. 140
5   Ibid., p. 152
6   Ibid., p. 185
7   Ibid., pp. 183–5
8   K.H. Jackson (ed. and trs.), *The Gododdin:
    The Oldest Scottish Poem*, Edinburgh,
    Edinburgh University Press, 1969
9   Anderson, 1980, p. 172
10 Sherley-Price, 1990, p. 146
11 Smyth, 1984, pp. 61–2 suggests that
    Talorgan son of Eanfrid and Drust son of
    Donnel, in particular, were puppet kings
    under Oswy
12 Sherley-Price, 1990, pp. 74–6
13 Ibid., p. 118
14 Ibid., p. 203
15 Ibid., pp. 308–21
16 Ibid., p. 186
17 Ibid., p. 189
18 Ibid., p. 170
19 Ibid., pp. 196–200
20 Skene, 1867, pp. 71, 350
21 B. Colgrave (trs.), *Eddius Stephanus: The
    Life of Bishop Wilfrid*, Cambridge,
    Cambridge University Press, 1927, pp. 41,
    43

22 Ibid., p. 43
23 Smyth, 1984, p. 62
24 Anderson, 1980, p. 172
25 Colgrave, 1927, pp. 43, 45
26 Ibid, pp. 49, 51 (for his wealth, see also pp. 45 and 137)
27 Sherley-Price, 1990, pp. 224–5
28 Ibid., pp. 254–5
29 Ibid., p. 328; Skene, 1867, pp. 73, 352

Chapter 13

1 Bede devoted a whole chapter (21) to Nechtan's conversion to the Roman Easter (Sherley-Price, 1990, pp. 308–21)
2 Sherley-Price, 1990, Chapter 22, pp. 321–2; Skene, 1867, pp. 74, 354
3 Smyth, 1984, p. 75
4 Dated events recorded by the Irish annalists and referred to in this chapter are given by Skene, 1867, pp. 73–6 (Annals of Tigernach) and pp. 353–8 (Annals of Ulster)
5 See Chapter 3
6 The tangled history of the kings of Dalriada in this period is detailed by Anderson, 1980, pp. 179–88
7 Skene, 1867, pp. 76, 358; Morris, 1980, p. 47
8 Anderson, 1980, pp. 185, 189
9 Even the Group A versions of the *Pictish Chronicle* are not in complete agreement for this period. The 971–95 copy omitted the reign of Talorcen son of Drosten (presumably a scribal error), while the later copies give longer reigns for Bredei son of Wirguist (15 years) and Talorcen son of Drostan (12½ years). The table presented gives the reign lengths most easily reconciled with the dates given by the Irish annalists

Chapter 14

1 Anderson, 1980, pp. 191, 200
2 Fergus and Eochoid are listed in the *Synchronisms of Flann Mainistreach* (Skene, 1867, pp. 20–1), but are omitted from the *Duan Albanach* (Skene, 1867, p. 61), presumably because of the loss of a verse from the poem (Anderson, 1980, p. 45)
3 Anderson, 1980, p. 46, n. 11
4 Skene, 1867, p. 10
5 Ibid., p. 8
6 Ibid., pp. 203, 299

7 If Kenneth mac Alpin ruled for two years in Dalriada before beginning any part of his reign over the Picts, Wthoil son of Bargoit must already have been king of the Picts for about two years by the time Kenneth took power in Dalriada
8 Skene, 1867, p. 133
9 Only twice in the Group A versions, which do not include Kinat son of Ferat, one of the last kings to stand out against Kenneth's rule
10 In the Annals of Tigernach for 726, we read 'Dungal de regno ejectus est et Drust de regno Pictorum ejectus et Elphin pro eo regnat. Eochach mc Echach regnare incipit.' Following this, in 733, 'Eochach mac Echach Ri Dalriada et Conall mac Concobair mortui sunt' (Skene, 1867, pp. 74, 75)

Chapter 15

1 The page covering this period in the Annals of Tigernach is missing
2 Ritchie and Breeze, 1991, p. 37
3 Skene, 1867, p. 361
4 Smyth, 1984, p. 192
5 Skene, 1867, p. 405
6 Ibid., p. 58
7 Ibid., p. 169
8 Ibid., p. 117
9 Anderson, 1980, p. xvii
10 Skene, 1867, p. 135
11 Thorpe, 1966, p. 75
12 G. Donaldson, *Scottish Historical Documents*, Edinburgh, Scottish Academic Press, 1970, pp. 14–16
13 Skene, 1867, pp. 135–7

Chapter 16

1 Skene, 1867, pp. 58, 59
2 Ibid., p. 362
3 Ibid., pp. 130–4
4 Ibid., p. 21
5 Ibid., pp. 148–52
6 Ibid., pp. 171–6
7 Ibid, pp. 194–208
8 Thorpe, 1966, pp. 123–4
9 Skene, 1867, pp. 163–6; A.O. Anderson, *Early Sources of Scottish History AD 500 to 1286*, Edinburgh, Oliver and Boyd, Vol. 1, 1922, pp. 273–4
10 Thorpe, 1966, pp. 164–5
11 Morris, 1980, p. 32
12 Cummins, 1992, pp. 170–2

13 Skene, 1867, pp. 285–90. Skene, placing rather too much trust in the medieval 'facts and figures' (1867, p. lxv), dated this document to 1317

Chapter 17

1 A. Jackson, *The Symbol Stones of Scotland: A Social and Anthropological Resolution of the Problem of the Picts*, Stromness, Orkney Press, 1984
2 Nash-Williams, 1950
3 J. Close-Brooks, 'Pictish and Other Burials'; R. Gourlay, 'A Symbol Stone and Cairn at Watenan, Caithness'; L.M. MacLagan Wedderburn and D.M. Grime, The Cairn Cemetary at Garbeg, Drumnadrochit'; C. Thomas, 'The Pictish Class I Symbol Stones', in: Friell and Watson, 1984
4 Jackson, 1984, p. 19
5 Ibid, pp. 29–43
6 A somewhat similar line of argument was used by Dr Ross Sampson of Glasgow, but he came to the conclusion that it was the combinations of symbols that represented names, with the individual symbols presumably being a sort of syllabic alphabet. This hypothesis is discussed by E. Sutherland, *In Search of the Picts*, London, Constable, 1994 p. 81
7 Laing and Laing, 1993, pp. 95–7; A. Lane, 'Some Pictish Problems at Dunadd', in: Friell and Watson, 1984, pp. 45–7

Chapter 18

1 Ritchie and Breeze, 1991, pp. 51–3
2 A useful summary of the various interpretations of Sueno's Stone is given in a recent paper by D. Sellar, 'Sueno's Stone and its Interpreters', in: W.D.H. Sellar (ed.), *Moray: Province and People*, The Scottish Society for Northern Studies, 1993, pp. 96–116
3 Thorpe, 1966, pp. 123–4; Skene, 1867, pp. 122–3
4 Skene, 1867, pp. 156–7
5 Ibid., p. 199
6 Sherley-Price, 1990, p. 46
7 Skene, 1867, pp. 8–10
8 Ibid., pp. 361, 405
9 Ibid., p. 8
10 Ibid., pp. 405–7

Appendix 3

1 Wade Evans, 1938, pp. 101–2
2 H.M. Chadwick, 'Vortigern', in: H.M. Chadwick *et al.*, *Studies in Early British History*, Cambridge, Cambridge University Press, 1954, p. 27, n. 1
3 Skene, 1867, pp. 133–4, 144–5

Bibliography

Alcock, L. *Arthur's Britain: History and Archaeology*, London, Penguin, 1971.

Alcock, L. 'Pictish Studies: Present and Future', in A. Small (ed.) *The Picts: A New Look at Some Old Problems*, Dundee, 1987, pp. 80–92.

Anderson A.O. *Early Sources of Scottish History AD 500 to 1286*, 2 vols, Edinburgh, Oliver and Boyd, 1922.

Anderson, A.O. and Anderson, M.O. (eds and trs.) *Adomnan's Life of Columba*, London, Thomas Nelson, 1961.

Anderson, M.O. *Kings and Kingship in Early Scotland*, Edinburgh and London, Scottish Academic Press, 1980.

Cary, E. (trs.) *Dio's Roman History*, vol. 9, London, Heinemann, 1927.

Chadwick, H.M. 'Vortigern', in: H.M. Chadwick *et al.* (eds) *Studies in Early British History*, Cambridge, Cambridge University Press, 1954, pp. 21–46.

Close-Brooks, J. 'Pictish and Other Burials', in J.G.P. Friell and W.G. Watson (eds) *Pictish Studies: Settlement, Burial and Art in Dark Age Northern Britain*, British Archaeological Reports, 125, Oxford, 1984, pp. 87–114.

Close-Brooks, J. 'Excavations at Clatchard Craig, Fife', *Proceedings of the Society of Antiquaries of Scotland*, 116 (1986), 117–84.

Colgrave, B. (trs.) Eddius Stephanus: *The Life of Bishop Wilfrid*, Cambridge, Cambridge University Press, 1927.

Collingwood, R.G. and Myers, J.N.L. *Roman Britain and the English Settlements*, 2nd edn, Oxford, Clarendon Press, 1937.

Cummins, W.A. *King Arthur's Place in Prehistory: The Great Age of Stonehenge*, Stroud, Alan Sutton Publishing, 1992.

Donaldson, G. *Scottish Historical Documents*, Edinburgh, Scottish Academic Press, 1970.

Dumville, D. *et al. Saint Patrick, AD 493–1993*, Woodbridge, Boydell Press, 1993.

Frere, S. *Britannia: A History of Roman Britain*, London, Routledge and Kegan Paul, 3rd edn, 1987.

Friell, J.G.P. and Watson, W.G. (eds) *Pictish Studies: Settlement, Burial and Art in Dark Age Northern Britain*, British Archaeological Reports, 125, Oxford, 1984.

Garmonsway, G.N. (trs.) *Anglo-Saxon Chronicle*, London, Dent, 1953.

Gourlay, R. 'A Symbol Stone and Cairn at Watenan, Caithness', in J.G.P. Friell and W.G. Watson (eds) *Pictish Studies: Settlement Burial and Art in Dark Age Northern Britain*, British Archaeological Reports, 125, Oxford, 1984, pp. 131–3.

Graham-Campbell, J. 'Norrie's Law, Fife: On the Nature and Dating of the

Silver Hoard', *Proceedings of the Society of Antiquaries of Scotland*, 121 (1991), 241–59.

Henderson, I. *The Picts*, London, Thames and Hudson, 1967.

Higham, N.J. *The English Conquest: Gildas and Britain in the Fifth Century*, Manchester, Manchester University Press, 1994.

Hutton, M. (trs.) *Tacitus in Five Volumes*, vol. 1, pt 1, 'Agricola', London, Heinemann, 1980.

Jackson, A. *The Symbol Stones of Scotland: A Social Anthropological Resolution of the Problem of the Picts*, Orkney, Orkney Press, 1984.

Jackson, K.H. 'Common Gaelic: the Evolution of the Goedelic Languages', *Proceedings of the British Academy*, 37 (1951), 71–97.

Jackson, K.H. 'The Pictish Language', in F.T. Wainwright (ed.) *The Problem of the Picts*, Edinburgh, Thomas Nelson, 1956, pp. 129–66.

Jackson, K.H. (ed. and trs.) *The Gododdin: The Oldest Scottish Poem*, Edinburgh, Edinburgh University Press, 1969.

Johnston, J.B. *Place-names of Scotland*, Edinburgh, David Douglas, 1892.

Laing, L. and Laing, J. *The Picts and the Scots*, Stroud, Alan Sutton Publishing, 1993.

Laing, L. and Laing, J. 'The Date and Origin of the Pictish Symbols', *Proceedings of the Society of Antiquaries of Scotland*, 114 (1984), 261–76.

Lane, A. 'Some Pictish Problems at Dunadd', in J.G.P. Friell and W.G. Watson (eds) *Pictish Studies: Settlement Burial and Art in Dark Age Northern Britain*, British Archaeological Reports, 125, Oxford, 1984, pp. 43–62.

Macbain, A. 'Ptolomey's Geography of Scotland', *Transactions of the Gaelic Society of Inverness*, 18 (1892), 267–88.

MacLagan Wedderburn, L.M. and Grime, D.M. 'The Cairn Cemetery at Garbeg, Drumnadrochit', in J.G.P. Friell and W.G. Watson (eds) *Pictish Studies: Settlement Burial and Art in Dark Age Northern Britain*, British Archaeological Reports, 125, Oxford, pp. 151–67.

Metcalfe, W.M. *Pinkerton's Lives of the Scottish Saints*, rev. edn, vol. II, Paisley, Alexander Gardner, 1889.

Metcalfe, W.M. *The Legends of SS Ninian and Machor, from an Unique MS in the Scottish Dialect of the Fourteenth Century*, Paisley, Alexander Gardner, 1904.

Morris, J. *The Age of Arthur: A History of the British Isles from 350–650*, London, Weidenfeld and Nicolson, 1973.

Morris, J. (ed. and trs.) Nennius: *British History and the Welsh Annals*, London, Phillimore, 1980.

Nash-Williams, V.E. *The Early Christian Monuments of Wales*, Cardiff, University of Wales Press, 1950.

Nicolaisen, W.F.H. *Scottish Place-names: Their Study and Significance*, London, Batsford, 1976.

Oldfather, C.H. (trs.) *Diodorus of Sicily*, vol. III, London, Heinemann, 1939.

Renfrew, C. *British Prehistory: A New Outline*, London, Duckworth, 1974.

Ritchie, A. and Breeze, D.J. *Invaders of Scotland*, Edinburgh, HMSO, 1991.

Sellar, D. 'Sueno's Stone and its Interpreters', in: W.D.H. Sellar (ed.) *Moray: Province and People*, The Scottish Society for Northern Studies, 1993, pp. 96–116.

Sherley-Price, L. (trs.) Bede: *Ecclesiastical History of the English People with Bede's Letter to Egbert and Cuthbert's Letter on the Death of Bede*, rev. edn, Penguin, 1990.

Skene, W.F. (ed.) *Chronicles of the Picts, Chronicles of the Scots, and other Early Memorials of Scottish History*, Edinburgh, HM General Register House, 1867.

Small, A. (ed.) *The Picts: A New Look at Some Old Problems*, Dundee, 1987.

Smyth, A.P. *Warlords and Holy Men: Scotland AD 80–1000*, London, Edward Arnold, 1984.

Stenton, F.M. *Anglo-Saxon England*, 2nd edn, Oxford, Clarendon Press, 1947.

Stevenson, R.B.K. 'Pictish Chain, Roman Silver and Bauxite Beads', *Proceedings of the Society of Antiquaries of Scotland*, 88 (1956), 228–30.

Sutherland, E. *In Search of the Picts*, London, Constable, 1994.

Thomas, A.C. 'Excavations at Trusty's Hill, Anwoth, 1960', *Transactions of the Dumfries and Galloway Natural History and Archaeological Society*, 38 (1961), 58–70.

Thomas, C. 'The Pictish Class I Symbol Stones', in J.G.P. Friell and W.G. Watson (eds) *Pictish Studies: Settlement Burial and Art in Dark Age Northern Britain*, British Archaeological Reports, 125, Oxford, 1984, pp. 169–87.

Thorpe, L. (trs.) Geoffrey of Monmouth: *The History of the Kings of Britain*, London, Penguin, 1966.

Wade-Evans, A.W. (ed. and trs.) *Nennius: History of the Britons etc.*, London, Church Historical Society, new series 34, 1938.

Wainwright, F.T. 'The Picts and the Problem', in F.T. Wainwright (ed.) *The Problem of the Picts*, Edinburgh, Thomas Nelson, 1956, pp. 1–53.

Watkins, T. 'Where Were the Picts: An Essay in Settlement Archaeology', in J.G.P. Friell and W.G. Watson (eds) *Pictish Studies: Settlement, Burial and Art in Dark Age Northern Britain*, British Archaeological Reports, 125, Oxford, 1984, pp. 63–86.

Watson, W.J. *The History of the Celtic Place-names of Scotland*, Edinburgh, William Blackwood and Sons Ltd, 1926.

West, D. (trs.) Virgil: *The Aeneid*, London, Penguin, 1990.

Wheeler, R.E.M. *Maiden Castle, Dorset*, Report of the Research Committee of the Society of Antiquaries of London, XII, 1943.

Williams, A.H. *An Introduction to the History of Wales*, vol. I: *Prehistoric Times to 1063 AD*, Cardiff, University of Wales Press, 1969.

Winterbottom, M. (ed. and trs.) Gildas: *The Ruin of Britain and Other Works*, London, Phillimore, 1978.

Index

Numbers in italics are references to illustrations